The Fractured
# Metropolis

SUNY Series, the New Inequalities

A. Gary Dworkin, Editor

# The Fractured
# Metropolis

## Political Fragmentation
## and Metropolitan Segregation

Gregory R. Weiher

*State University of New York Press*

Published by
State University of New York Press, Albany

For information, address State University of New York
Press, State University Plaza, Albany, N.Y., 12246

Production by Diane Ganeles
Marketing by Dana Yanulavich

Library of Congress Cataloging-in-Publication Data

Weiher, Gregory.
    The fractured metropolis : political fragmentation and
metropolitan segregation / Gregory R. Weiher.
        p.    cm. — (SUNY series, the new inequalities)
    Includes bibliographical references and index.
    ISBN 0-7914-0564-8 (CH : alk. paper). — ISBN 0-7914-0565-6
(PH: alk. paper)
    1. Discrimination in housing—United States.   2. Metropolitan
areas—United States.   3. Suburbs—United States.   4. United
States–Administrative and political divisions.   I. Title.   II. Series:
SUNY series in the new equalities.
HD7288.76.U5W45 1991
363.5'1—dc20                                                    90–9878
                                                                    CIP

10 9 8 7 6 5 4 3 2 1

*To My Wife*

# Contents

# Preface

This book grows out of my experience as a research consultant to the St. Louis Board of Education while I was a graduate student at Washington University. When it was found to have maintained a segregated system of public schools, the board filed a cross-complaint against the twenty-three school districts in St. Louis County, claiming that they had contributed to segregation in the schools of the St. Louis School District. A small army of attorneys and social scientists was hired to examine the records of the county school districts for evidence of racially discriminatory activity.

Hours spent researching the organizational history of education in St. Louis County left the impression that an important element in the process of discrimination had been ignored. The focus of the effort on both sides was on establishing that whites had or had not taken direct actions against blacks. Researchers were asked to find answers to a number of questions:

—Had white educators in high school districts denied transfers of blacks from districts without high schools?

—Were black children provided with inferior educational facilities?

—Had county school districts discriminated against black teachers in hiring?

Questions such as these were important for understanding discrimination in the St. Louis area, but they addressed it only partially. Such a focus produces a record of incidents, but it does not detect the broader pattern.

The structuring of political space was far more important in determining the relationships of blacks and whites in the educational system than were particular discriminatory actions. The drawing and redrawing of political boundaries is a more subtle strategy than confrontation, but its effects are more pervasive and enduring. Indeed, if political boundaries are appropriately drawn, confrontation is not required to maintain racial separation.

The "second class citizen," though he or she may be relatively disadvantaged, may nevertheless gain some satisfaction by insisting upon the rights shared by all citizens. The *non*-citizen, one who is outside the political space, can make no claim upon the resources or guarantees of the polity, no matter how wretched may be his or her situation. Political boundaries that give geographic manifestation to racial antipathies permit citizenship to be manipulated to serve racial purposes. In the St. Louis area, for instance, blacks frequently have no rights as citizens in those school districts which are rich in educational resources.

In the St. Louis metropolitan area, school district boundaries were very frequently racial boundaries also. Until the 1960s, most black children attended schools in St. Louis City. Black children living in the county were enrolled in majority-black districts such as Kinloch and Scudder. Even today, this coincidence of racial and political boundaries persists. School districts that appear to be integrated at some point in time—Berkeley, Ferguson-Florissant, Kirkwood—are in the midst of racial transition, and will soon be all black, if they are not already.

This coincidence of racial and political boundaries is more consequential for segregation and inequalities of opportunity than the particular actions, taken by whites against blacks, that we were directed to look for in the St. Louis school desegregation case. Furthermore, segregation of this sort is more secure against attack. The Supreme Court has in most cases found that segregation that occurs at a political boundary requires no legal remedy.

Why should this situation, in which political boundaries are also racial boundaries, persist? Municipalities can employ land-use controls to pursue segregation, but school districts have no such power. How is segregation across school district boundaries maintained? Is the mere existence of a political boundary enough to support segregation?

These are the preoccupations of this book. It argues that the bounding of political space permits an interaction of geography, demography, and human cognition which tends to result in segregation by race and class. The existence of a boundary, particularly one which is unambiguous and authoritatively established, distinguishes one place from another. In turn, such places can be cognitively differentiated by persons seeking suitable locations in metropolitan areas. Because suitability is often defined in terms of the racial and class identity of the people that live in particular places, political boundaries can become socioeconomic boundaries also. That is, political boundaries can become social fractures.

This book could not have been finished without the generosity of a great many people. I am heavily indebted to Robert Salisbury, John Sprague, Lucius Barker, Paul Johnson, and George Tsebelis. I have received very good advice on particular parts of this book from John McIver, James Stimson, Robert Stein, and Kent Tedin. I am grateful to all of these people, and to the members of the political science departments of Washington University in St. Louis and the University of Houston.

Most of all, I am grateful to my wife.

Of course, I have chosen not to accept some of the excellent advice that these people have offered, and so there are many faults in the finished product. For these, I am responsible.

# 1

## Urban Political Boundaries and Metropolitan Fragmentation

I try to convince my students in American Government, State Government, and Urban Politics that the United States is the most fragmented country in the world.

The task is made more difficult by the fact that my contention cannot be proven. So many of the units which are the stuff of American fragmentation have no counterpart in other countries. Tricks of language and definition deprive us of confidence in our comparisons even when we think we have found entities which are comparable across nations. So, when the Department of the Census (1982a) declares that there are 82,341 units of government in the United States, I cannot prove to my students that that is more units of government than exist in any other country—it is not clear that all other countries keep track of such things, nor that "government" and "unit of government" mean the same thing in all countries and all languages. But it is my decided judgement that this is so.

"Consider," I say to them, "the number of McDonald's Restaurants in the world." I use this reference for two reasons—McDonald's is a palpable presence for almost all university students, and everyone knows that McDonald's are like grains of sand or like stars in the heavens. As nearly as I can tell, there are about 8,000 McDonald's in

1

the world. I point out to my students that there are not one tenth as many McDonald's in the world as there are governments in the United States, and they are duly impressed.

The evidence of our fragmentation is not only governmental. I suspect that the United States has more organized religious denominations than any country in the world. One source reports that there are more than ten thousand organizations that employ lobbyists to pursue their interests at the federal level alone (Prewitt, Verba, and Salisbury 1987). We have experienced massive waves of immigration, making us, if not the most ethnically diverse of countries, certainly as diverse as any other.

We have been fragmented by design as well as happenstance. I would argue that a close reading of Federalist 10 and 51 can support no other conclusion than that American government is intended to be as inefficient as it can possibly be while still maintaining a pretense of organization.

Indeed, I think that fragmentation in the United States, social, political, and economic, is neither random nor inconsequential. Rather, I think that fragmentation is one of the obdurate facts of American society and culture, and that diverse manifestations of fragmentation in every facet of American life have a symphonic relationship to one another. Fragmentation speaks to the essence of our national character, is perhaps the best indication of what we value, and explains a great many social and political outcomes.

Governmental fragmentation at the local level is Jeffersonian in its theoretical origins. Jefferson's commitment to a ward system in which local governments perform the bulk of governmental functions, with higher units becoming progressively less active, is familiar to students of American political thought. The local government was to be the incubator of democracy, training citizens in their rights and responsibilities. Honesty, immediacy, and responsiveness were taken to be the virtues of government close to the people. The American experience of decentralized self-government embodied in the New England town reinforced the Jeffersonian predilection.

Institutional and legal practice soon were brought into conformity with the localist impulse in the independent United States (Teaford 1979). At first, the legislatures of the states reviewed petitions for incorporation singly. As such petitions became more numerous, however, the ability of the legislatures to legislate was impeded. Early on, the pattern of automatic state sanction for incorporations that conformed to certain objective criteria was established. If it could be shown that a proposed municipality would exceed a minimum population requirement, and if a majority of residents of the proposed corporation approved its creation in a plebiscite, then state approval would be forthcoming. This is the legal structure of the creation of units of government that persists today. The creation of units of local government is, for the most part, not supervised by any central governmental unit. Local governments in the United States exist almost entirely as a matter of local volition (Miller 1981; Mowitz and Wright 1962).

This lack of central supervision over government creation may be another unique feature of the United States. Teaford compares practice in the United States with that in the United Kingdom. In the United Kingdom, communities wishing to incorporate must petition an agency of national government. Thus begins a lengthy process of study and deliberation which attempts to determine, among other things, if the community has sufficient population to warrant its own political identity; if the community has the economic resources to support the services and activities incumbent upon government; and if there are no other political entities in the area which might undertake such services and activities so that the creation of an additional unit of government might be avoided. Berry (1973) also emphasizes the relatively decentralized nature of urban development in the United States compared to other industrialized Western nations. Western Europe and the United Kingdom have a long history of urban planning. Land use and community formation are under public, central control to a much greater extent than they are in the United States. Even in those instances when the creation of suburban communities is encouraged as a matter of national policy, as with the British New Towns program, the French *Schema Directeur,* the Finnish Seven Towns Plan, or the Swedish Master Plan for Stockholm, it is to serve national and public purposes of equalizing economic development, providing services equably, redistributing wealth, and ameliorating housing shortages. Local prerogative is not a high priority.

In this book, "political fragmentation" refers to the proliferation of governments across American society and geography. It denotes the division of urban areas among hundreds of overlapping, autonomous political units, each with an array of powers—regulation, taxation, incarceration, program implementation, allocation of public resources. . . .

Can it be that the pervasiveness of political fragmentation in the United States has no practical significance? Can a country which is so socially diverse and politically and economically fragmented be unremarkable? Perhaps this diversity and fragmentation is simply a curiosity, an interesting trait of Americans to be remarked upon in travel guides in the same way that we remark that certain native peoples in Africa are extraordinarily tall, or wear bones in their noses.

To the extent that fragmentation is a matter of design, however, it must have been meant to accomplish something. Madison argues that an extended, socially diverse—one might say, pluralistic—republic and a government in which the power of factions is divided and balanced are likely to protect the rights of the people. If no faction can gain a monopoly over the power and apparatus of government, the state cannot be used to deprive the people of their freedom and property. Half of Madison's vision has been realized in a society which is diverse and a governmental structure in which it is easier to veto action than to pursue it to its culmination.

The ability of this structure to guarantee equal freedom and distribute rewards equably to the citizens has
been questioned, however. Some would argue that plural-
ism rewards those who already have resources (Schattschneider 1975; Macpherson 1962, 1977), and that the
checks and balances built into American government are
more likely to preserve the privileges of the few than to
protect the freedoms of the many. The existence of thou-
sands of units of local government certainly divides power,
if our perspective is national. If our perspective is local,
however, the multiplication of local governments is also
the progressive entrenchment of power. The atomization of
potential national majorities is the simultaneous institu-
tionalization of majorities at the local level. The result
may be something different than the thriving cells of democracy envisioned by Jefferson. The result may only be a
system of structured inequalities.

This is a book about political fragmentation in the
United States. It is specifically about metropolitan areas
and about the number of political jurisdictions that exist
in American metropolitan areas. In this regard it is not
unique. Other books have also addressed the subject of political fragmentation in American metropolitan areas
(Danielson 1972, 1976; Miller 1981; Norton 1979; Teaford
1979), and social scientists have produced an immense
amount of literature dealing with the implications of this
extreme fragmentation. Of particular concern have been
the implications of fragmentation for questions of efficiency and equality. In addressing these questions, some
analysts are led to call for reforms in the structure of local
governance on the grounds of the inequalities that fragmentation generates or the inefficiencies it visits upon
the pursuit of public purposes. Others feel that these inequalities are exaggerated, or that far from causing ineffi-
ciency, governmental fragmentation and overlap promote
flexibility and efficiency in the allocation of resources. Despite this diversity of perspectives, all of these analyses
have one thing in common—they are essentially concerned with institutional factors. The debate centers on

the actions and powers of governments. The crux of the
debate is what governments do, or how their powers are
used by particular groups. To the extent that the geographic structure of metropolitan fragmentation is mentioned, it is only in passing.

The intent of this book is to reverse these priorities to
see what follows. Behind this strategy is the conviction
that the least ambiguous facet of metropolitan fragmentation is that it is structured by political boundaries. In
turn, the least ambiguous function of these boundaries is
to demarcate discrete spatial units. I argue that proceed-
ing upon these bases, it is possible to reproduce many of
the results that are usually explained by invoking institutional factors.

Ultimately, of course, this discussion has policy implications. The way in which we understand urban governmental fragmentation will have its impact on policy
regarding the contours and processes of local governance.
If many of the outcomes we attribute to institutional factors actually result from political boundary structures,
policies that are meant to modify these outcomes can have
only limited success while boundary structures are intact.

## Suburbanization and its Social Implications

In the years after World War II suburbanization became irresistable. Pent up demand for new housing along
with FHA and VA loan policies and improved transportation systems promoted tremendous growth at the urban
periphery (Campbell and Meranto 1971). These developments have been well documented and need not be examined in detail here (Teaford 1979; Berry 1973: 35–36;
Danielson 1976: 201–205; Orfield 1976).

By the 1950s, then, suburbanization and urban fragmentation had become a formative social process in the
American experience, one of those developments that impinges upon such a wide variety of affairs and endeavors
that it reshapes the contours of society. A burgeoning so-

cial science literature began to consider seriously the implications of the changing form of the metropolis.

There was an early understanding that the growth of the suburbs had effects that were not neutral with regard to classes and strata. It has been widely recognized that suburban expansion is more than a function of urban population growth; that it is in many cases driven by class and racial antipathies as well as by simple numbers (Berry 1973: chapter 2; Judd 1979: chapter 6; Farley 1976; Danielson 1976: chapter 1). Two trends are apparent from analyses of the sociological component of suburban growth: first, it has resulted in broad socioeconomic differences between the cities and the suburbs; and second, socioeconomic differences have emerged among suburbs that tend to be jurisdictionally structured.

In the period immediately following World War II, the larger American central cities typically experienced either a decline in population growth or an absolute decline in population. These declines were almost always coupled with increasing suburban growth rates (Berry 1973; Schnore et al. 1976; Sternlieb and Hughes 1976). The experience of St. Louis is representative of this trend. The population of the city of St. Louis peaked in 1950 at about 850,000. From 1950 to 1980, this figure has been reduced by half, while the population of surrounding St. Louis County has increased substantially (Schmandt, Wendel, and Tomey 1983; B. Williams 1973). A similar process has taken place in Chicago (Orlebeke 1983) and New York (Gordon 1976; Sternlieb and Hughes 1976). Nor have the cities of the West been entirely exempt, as indicated by demographic trends in Los Angeles and surrounding counties (Miller 1981: 172–176; Schnore et al. 1976).

Much of the increase in suburban population is the result of emigration from the urban core (Downs 1981: 2). This emigration has not been random respecting the characteristics of the emigres. Definite trends are identifiable with regard to the sorts of people who are likely to move from city to suburb. Such persons tend to be white, younger, better educated, and more affluent than the persons who remain in central cities (Schnore, Andre, and Sharp 1976; Kasarda 1983; Schmandt, Wendell, and Tomey 1979; Schultze et al. 1976; Sternlieb and Hughes 1976; Campbell and Meranto 1971).

Though the suburbs are, on average, distinguishable from the central cities, one should not conclude that there is no variation between suburban jurisdictions themselves. A great deal of socioeconomic, demographic, and cultural variety exists in suburbia, and a number of observers have noticed that it is spatially structured. Suburban political units tend not only to be spatially and jurisdictionally distinct, but to be identifiable in terms of the compositions and life styles of their populations as well.

The most prominent characteristic distinguishing suburban jurisdictional populations is race, and segregation by this characteristic is more complete than by any other. In those areas where blacks do move from central cities to suburbs, it is predominantly to suburbs that are contiguous with central city ghettoes (Orfield 1978: 51; Berry et al. 1976: 236–242; Danielson 1976: 8; Massey and Mullan 1984; Stahura 1988). These are the suburbs with the oldest housing, weakest city services and tax bases, and highest bonded indebtedness (Massey and Denton 1988a; Schneider and Logan 1982). Furthermore, the suburbs in which blacks live are not in any meaningful sense "integrated." Danielson notes:

> As a result of these settlement patterns, most suburbs have only a handful of black residents, while a few have large minority populations. Almost 7,000 of the 10,000 blacks in Southern California's Orange County resided in Santa Ana in 1970, compared with 170 in Anaheim and 41 in Newport Beach, where they comprised 0.1 percent and 0.08 percent of the population respectively. In northern New Jersey, 89 percent of Essex County's 72,000 black residents in 1970 lived in East Orange, Orange, and Montclair—all older suburbs bordering on Newark. Fifteen of the 237 suburban munici-

palities in the Chicago area accounted in 1970 for 83
percent of the 128,300 blacks living in the suburbs.
Moreover, as Pierre De Vise has pointed out, the Chicago area's "entire 10-year gain of 50,000 suburban
blacks during the 1960s occurred in these fifteen suburbs" (Danielson 1976: 8–9).

What is true of municipalities holds for school districts as well (Orfield 1978: 75–76). Those suburban jurisdictions in which intermediate proportions of blacks do
occur are usually in the midst of rapid and inexorable
transition from black to white (Orfield 1978: 93). Berry
and his co-authors have touched upon the dynamic underlying the ubiquitous occurrence of racial transition. Following Taeuber and Taeuber (1965: 112), they point out
that housing occupied by blacks rarely reverts to white
ownership. "When an 'integrated neighborhood' was defined as one attracting both blacks and whites, a national
survey found a median black population of only 3% in
such neighborhoods." (Berry et al. 1976: 222).

Considerations such as these lead Orfield to conclude
that "in United States society, physical separation is reinforced by race, a bitter history of race relations, and an
increasing tendency for political boundaries to become racial boundaries" (Orfield 1976: 381).

Suburban political jurisdictions have also been found
to differ along a number of other dimensions. Distinctions
by class, defined roughly in terms of wealth and income,
are present, though they are not as rigidly structured as
racial differences (Miller 1981: chapter 6; Danielson 1976:
5–14; Hill 1974; Logan 1983; Logan and Schneider 1981).
Differences in a wide variety of population characteristics
were found by Schnore (1971) to vary with the economic
characteristics of suburbs. Dye and colleagues found that
suburbs vary by socioeconomic status and that these variations are important for differences in attitudes, policies,
and levels of cooperation in the delivery of services
(Williams and others 1971; Dye and others 1971). Perhaps
the broadest category by which suburban jurisdictions

have been found to vary is that of "life style" or "culture". This category incorporates considerations of income, occupation, education, and sometimes race, ethnicity, and religion. Jurisdictional segregation by life style is at the base of what Berry terms "the mosaic culture" (Berry 1973: 64–66), and Williams argues that life style differences across suburbs are crucial in understanding the fragmentation of metropolitan government itself. Local governments, according to Williams, are willing to surrender autonomy over routine system-maintenance functions; but they zealously guard their autonomy over policies governing areas such as housing and education that impinge upon the life style values of the community (Williams 1980).

A substantial literature, then, supports the conclusion that there is considerable differentiation by political unit along a number of dimensions—race, occupation, education, income, and composite measures of socioeconomic status and life style—among metropolitan jurisdictions. This conclusion is rarely contested.

Recent work by E. Ostrom (1983) provides one of these rare examples. Ostrom notes that a good deal of stratification by political unit exists (p. 92), but that its significance may be overestimated. Though there are small, homogeneous rich and poor suburbs in almost every metropolitan area, these polar examples are not representative of the broader array of jurisdictions. She cites the work of Logan and Schneider which asserts that the "extent to which residential segregation actually is found is often overstated" (1981: 24).

This disagreement over the extent of jurisdictional segregation by income group (Ostrom agrees that the races are jurisdictionally segregated) is in great part semantical. As one group of observers notes, ". . . neighborhood homogeneity is clearly a relative concept; there is no doubt that 'homogenous' neighborhoods contain a population with an often broad range of occupations, educational backgrounds, and even class affiliations" (Berry et al. 1976: 254).

The problem, then, is to determine at what point we can consider a given jurisdictional population significantly different from others. Indeed, the widespread use of the term "homogeneity" in this context is misleading in that it makes a stronger claim than most analysts intend. I would rather speak of jurisdictional "eccentricity". Webster tells us that eccentricity occurs when spheres do not have the same center. Eccentricity is "a deviation from an established pattern, rule, or norm" (G. and C. Merriam Company 1966: 261). It is useful to appropriate the term in this context to compare jurisdictional populations with MSA populations or county populations. When jurisdictional means deviate substantially from the means of greater populations, such deviant jurisdictions are described as "eccentric". This is a more accurate term than "homogeneity" because it indicates not that the composition of the population is uniform, but that it is distinguishable from others in terms of the distribution of some characteristic.

Schneider and Logan base their claim (that the distinctiveness of suburbs is overstated) on their use of a two-to-one ratio of poverty or wealth. That is, if a suburb has twice as great a proportion of poor or wealthy families as the metropolitan proportion, it is considered significantly different from other suburbs. By their own standard, Schneider and Logan find 393 of 1,139 suburbs, or 34%, to be distinctive. One questions the givenness of the 2:1 ratio for determining distinctiveness. Why is it necessary for a suburb to have 100% more poor or rich families than the average for it to be considered distinctive? Is a suburb not socioeconomically distinct if it has 75% more rich or poor families than the metropolitan average? Of the 746 suburbs which have "a normal mixture of income classes," we might wonder about the relationship of the poorest to the wealthiest. What are the differences in income, property value, and proportion of home-ownership in these communities?

Schneider and Logan's use of the 2:1 standard is not unreasonable, but many standards and dimensions of inequality might reasonably inform judgements concerning the distinctiveness of suburbs. For instance, the finding reported in chapter 4 is that in suburban Cook and Los

Angeles Counties, more variance in racial composition, education, and occupation occurs among suburban municipalities than within them. Furthermore, any determination about the distinctiveness or lack thereof of suburbs should be made with an eye to the implications of differences in race and socioeconomic status for quality of life, provision of services, and life outcomes. Much previous work, for instance, supports the conclusion that differences in socioeconomic status are correlated with differences in services offered by suburbs (Williams et al. 1971; Dye et al. 1971). There are substantial differences in educational services offered by school districts in metropolitan areas, and these difference correlate closely with the socioeconomic status of residents (Berke, Goertz, and Coley 1984; Wise 1967).

The 2:1 standard offered by Schneider and Logan and, in turn, by Ostrom, appears somewhat arbitrary, and is an incomplete measure of suburban eccentricity in that it does not include race and other important characteristics. The preponderence of the social science literature concerning the sociology of the suburbs has been concerned with their social and economic distinctiveness, not with their uniformity (Stein 1987; Schnore 1972; Dye et al. 1971; Williams 1968). The arguments made by Ostrom, and by Schneider and Logan are not yet sufficient to justify discarding this literature, particularly when Logan and Schneider find in related research (1981) that income inequality in the suburbs of a majority of American cities appears to be increasing.

## Explanations of Suburban Eccentricity

Several explanations have been offered for the eccentricity of suburban populations. In this section, three of them are discussed—the "politics of exclusion", public choice, and neighborhood tipping. Each of these explanations has something to offer, but is for present purposes incomplete. The discussion of these explanations is meant as a preparation for the introduction of a theory of urban political boundaries and the ways in which they influence segregation by race and socioeconomic attributes, as well as other characteristics, in suburbs. Toward that end, Hirschman's treatment of exit behavior is also discussed (Hirschman 1970).

## The Politics of Exclusion

Exclusionary practices have been frequently cited as a cause of segregation by class and race (Danielson 1976; Frieden 1979; Cion 1971; Norton 1979; Miller 1981; Logan and Schneider 1984). This argument would have it that relatively homogeneous communities use political boundaries as defenses against low income and minority intruders.

The first step in acquiring exclusionary powers is to reinforce community identity politically through incorporation (Danielson 1976; Miller 1981; Cion 1971: 228; Mowitz and Wright 1962). Incorporation gives the community autonomy over land use and construction, and over the provision of services that may be essential to expanded development. Zoning ordinances, for instance, may prohibit the construction of all but single family dwellings on large lots. The cost of such housing precludes purchase by many of the types of people that suburbanites frequently consider undesirable. Exclusionary mechanisms have been extensively discussed elsewhere and need not be examined in detail here (Danielson 1976). That communities actually do incorporate toward such ends is not in dispute (See *The New York Times,* 1974).

In addition to politically acquired powers, residents frequently resort to open hostility and violence to frighten off intruders (Berry et al. 1976; Darnton 1974; Hirsch 1983). The exclusionary efforts of localities have been complemented by federal government policies in the underwriting of mortgages and the location of public and subsidized housing (Danielson 1976; Orfield 1976; Downs 1981). Additionally, realtors and lending institutions frequently route minority group members away from white communities (Danielson 1976; Orfield 1976; Downs 1981).

The existence of these practices is often invoked as a means of understanding stratification by jurisdiction. This explanation is at best partial, however. It demonstrates how certain types of persons are kept out of certain communities; but it says nothing about the way in which communities attract new settlers that are acceptable to them. The exclusion that occurs at a boundary cannot account for the persistence of homogeneous or eccentric communities in the presence of steady turnover in community membership (Downs 1981: 24–26, 35). For that, a process of recruitment or selection is required as a complement to exclusion. Not only must the wrong people be kept out, but the right people must be recruited to replace those who inevitably will defect.

Not surprisingly, the literature on exclusionary politics has not included a well articulated treatment of the recruitment function. There is implicit recognition that such a function exists. Berry and others, for instance, make the following statement: "Because Park Forest had been well publicized as an integrated community and many of the suburbs around it are known to be highly resistant to black immigration, increasing numbers of blacks began to seek homes within its confines" (1976: 241). There is a clear assumption here that recruitment of black families into Park Forest is occurring. But the implications of this process are not explored. We understand, therefore, that a recruitment dynamic is in place, but its articulation and implications have yet to be explored with the same thoroughness as the exculsionary dynamic.

Perhaps the best example of explicit interest in the recruitment function on the part of "exclusionists" is their attention to the role of the realtor in the sorting process. Realtors are clearly involved in the politics of exclusion by virtue of their practice of steering minority group members and persons of low socioeconomic status away from white, middle class neighborhoods (Danielson 1976: 12; Orfield 1976; Molotch 1972). More important here, however, are the techniques used by realtors for attracting persons with certain socioeconomic characteristics to housing areas that the realtor deems suitable for them (Judd 1979: 169–74). These techniques range from advertising in local media to supplying information to prospective buyers on the demographic and socioeconomic compositions of neighborhoods.

This explanation of recruitment is not satisfactory, however, because it provokes another question rather than providing an answer. If settlers of the appropriate type are recruited into communities by information supplied to them by realtors, where do realtors get their information? Do realtors use a different frame of reference in organizing information about metropolitan areas than other people might use? Is their information available only to the priesthood of realtors or is it information that any attentive person might obtain?

Suffice it to say that the exclusionist treatment of recruitment is for the most part oblique. One must look elsewhere for a more self-conscious treatment of jurisdictional recruitment.

## Urban Fragmentation and Public Choice

In a 1972 article, Elinor Ostrom offered the political economy approach as an alternative to the metropolitan reform traditions of urban analysis (Ostrom 1980). In that article, she discussed the principal assumptions of urban political economists (for a similar discussion, see Bish 1971: 1–17). Central among these assumptions are that the individual will make decisions so as to maximize his/her welfare (Ostrom 1980: 322). Political economists also assume that publicly provided goods and services have different characteristics, such that they will be best provided by governments that differ in the comprehensiveness of their jurisdictions and that are at different levels in the American federal system. This is an approach well suited for analyzing the decisions underlying recruitment. The basic analytical framework of the political economists consists of individuals with various locational preferences confronted by a variety of jurisdictions offering distinct service packages, each at a different cost. The sorting out of the population occurs when persons with certain preferences choose to locate in jurisdictions with particular service-cost combinations.

The classical statement of this model is Tiebout's (1956). He argues that the existence of multiple jurisdictions ameliorates the chief problem in the provision of public goods. When a settler chooses to live in a particular jurisdiction, s/he in effect reveals a preference for a particular bundle of services at a particular cost. This arrangement promotes the provision of public goods at optimal levels, increasing allocational efficiency by channeling resources to their most highly valued uses. In effect, fragmented local government imposes a market structure upon the provision of public goods. "The consumer may be viewed as picking that community which best satisfies his preference pattern for public goods. . . . the greater the variety among [communities], the closer the consumer will come to fully realizing his preference position" (Tiebout, 1956: 118).

The Tiebout model has had an enduring intuitive appeal. Its fundamental assumptions have informed a number of subsequent analyses (Bish 1971, 1976; Hawkins 1976; V. Ostrom, Warren, and Tiebout 1970). Though many of the assumptions of the model are naive (perfect mobility, complete absence of externalities), Tiebout has isolated the rudiments of a dynamic that is so plausible that we are convinced that it must somehow be at work in metropolitan areas. Subsequent analyses (Stein 1987; Lowery and Lyons 1989) continue to mine Tiebout's initial insight. Writing twenty-five years later, Peterson incorporates much of Tiebout's market logic into his argument about the limitations of city politics: ". . . the closer any locality moves toward the ideal match between taxes and services, the more attractive a setting it is for residents and the more valuable its land becomes" (Peterson 1981: 37).

The Tiebout model, then, supplies an argument about recruitment. Settlers find their ways to those government units that offer service/tax configurations closest to the ones that they prefer. In this context, however, assumption two of the model becomes specially interesting: "Consumer-voters are assumed to have full knowledge of differences among revenue and expenditure patterns . . ." (Tiebout 1956: 419). This assumption seems innocuous enough— that is, of course, until one recalls the number of government units that may be involved in the delivery of services to a single household.

Depending upon what are usually idiosyncratic considerations of governmental structure, residents may simultaneously receive services from a county, a municipality, a school district, a fire-protection district, a sewage treatment district, a health-and-sanitation district, a transportation authority, and so on. Scott and Corzine note that "San Mateo County, for example, has well over 400 different code areas for taxing purposes with approximately 75 special districts performing 8 to 12 different functions" (Scott and Corzine 1971). Conditions such as these are reproduced in metropolitan areas across the country. St. Louis County has ninety municipalities and twenty-four school districts among its 289 units of government. Harris County (Texas) includes within its boundaries upwards of 300 independent water districts (Perrenod 1984).

Given the complex structure of local government, the warrantability of granting the assumption of full knowledge on the part of consumers is questionable. It is a real chore for settlers to know simply the set of jurisdictions in which some location falls. Knowledge of the full variety of taxes levied in that location may not be easily gained (Scott and Corzine 1971: 204–206). Even more difficult will be the task of identifying each of the services that taxes purchase, not to mention determining the quality and level at which they are provided. Recent research (Lowery and Lyons 1989) suggests that citizens are not sufficiently aware of local government to be in possession of such detailed knowledge.

The question of consumer knowledge is not trivial. What these observations indicate is that theories of recruitment must make reference to the role of information. The following questions must be addressed: (1) how do consumers impose cognitive structures on metropolitan geographies in order to have some conception of differences between places? and (2) how do these structures condition the locational choices that they make?

The least satisfying aspect of the political economy approach to urban fragmentation is its myopia with respect to exclusionary practices and discrimination manifested in the unquestioning acceptance by political economists of the market as the ultimate, legitimate arbiter of urban locational outcomes. According to the Tiebout model and its articulators, fragmentation in metropolitan government is desirable because it fosters a quasi-market system for delivering public services.

A democratic society may value a number of things in addition to allocative efficiency, however. The problem with this market arrangement is that it permits wealth to determine the enjoyment of benefits that we might wish to be distributed independent of economic status. We might not want the quality of police and fire protection, education, and certain aspects of health to depend upon an individual's ability to buy into a desirable community (see Okun 1975: 1–32; Walzer 1980; Spitz 1977). Miller summarizes this line of criticism by saying ". . . I would maintain that efficiency is not a sufficient normative basis for making policy recommendations regarding metropolitan organization, despite the fact that that is the only normative criterion that is specifically mentioned by Tiebout himself and most of his followers" (Miller 1981: 187–88).

Part of this myopia is the assumption that the workings of markets are in themselves innocent—that they work in accord with immutable laws of supply and demand and are therefore divorced from normative considerations. In light of the work done on the politics of exclusion, this assumption is questionable. There is abundant evidence that residents of suburban jurisdictions purposefully structure markets to discriminate on social rather than economic grounds. Their intent is to see that locations not only go to the highest bidder, but that that bidder be middle class and white. It is true that discriminatory motives can be capitalized into real estate values and thus be given an economic representation. This does not alter the fact, however, that under these circumstances the market is primarily an instrument of status discrimination, whatever ostensibly economic functions it may perform.

## Neighborhood Tipping Models

A great deal of literature indicates that once black penetration of geographic units occurs, complete transition and succession is nearly inevitable (Massey and Mullan 1984; Berry et al. 1976; Duncan and Duncan 1957). The repeatedly demonstrated instability of integrated neighborhoods has prompted a number of analysts to offer the "neighborhood-tipping" explanation of neighborhood racial change (Steinnes 1977; Grodzins 1957; Schelling 1978; see also Taub, Taylor, and Dunham 1984; Stinchcombe, Mcdill and Walker 1969; Pryor 1971). According to this theory, once the proportion black of the population of a spatial unit reaches a certain point, an irreversible process of neighborhood transition is engendered.

Neighborhood tipping models are of interest here because they are predicated on the existence of discrete spatial units, and because they explain population dynamics in terms of the aggregate effects of individual decisions. Suburban municipalities and school districts *are* discrete spatial units (indeed, I would argue that they are considerably more discrete than the neighborhoods to which the tipping argument is usually addressed), and as such would seem to provide the necessary substratum upon which to build tipping point models.

The motivating forces behind the population dynamic described by tipping-point models are the perceptions and preferences of the residents of discrete spatial units (Schelling 1978). Whites have varying thresholds of toleration for blacks in their residential unit. As blacks move into the unit, whites with the lowest levels of tolerance move out, making more vacancies into which blacks can move. When blacks move into these vacancies, those who would have remained in the unit at the original level of black occupancy rethink their commitment, and some of them move, creating further vacancies. This structure of preferences and interdependent decision-making insures that a very small original penetration of a spatial unit by blacks is sufficient to tip it from all white to all black.

Tipping-point models are clearly based on a theory of recruitment (or perhaps it is more accurate to say a theory of recruitment and *dis*recruitment). People choose to leave spatial units based on their preferences about their neighbors. Though tipping point theorists talk mostly about exit, they imply also that those who leave will choose to live only in units in which they find their prospective neighbors desirable—that they will be recruited by such units. As such, they provide at least a partial complement to exclusionary theorists. They also supplement the work of political economists by pointing to additional preferences concerning neighbors and life style which are probably as important in determining residential choices as are concerns over service bundles and taxes. Finally, tipping theory provides an explanation for the racial distinctiveness that characterizes the populations of suburbs, implying that integrated municipalities or school districts should be inherently unstable, and that the majority of such spatial units at any point in time should be either all white or all black.

As with the work of the political economists, however, tipping models beg the question of information. Preferences about residence, whether they concern publicly provided goods and services or the racial and class characteristics of neighbors, can only be exercised when information about such things is available. As does Tiebout, however, tipping-point theorists tend to address the question of information by including it as an assumption in the articulation of their models.

One particularly important piece of information required by the decision-makers envisioned by tipping models is the location of the boundary of the spatial unit. The concept of tipping itself is meaningless without a prior assumption that there are discrete spatial units to be tipped. Absent a clearly defined and accessible boundary, the model becomes nonsense, as there are no bases for assigning racial identities to one place or another, and hence no criteria for moving or staying put. Indeed, one wonders what "moving" can mean without the prior existence of boundaries to distinguish places.

It is no accident, then, that part of Schelling's discussion of tipping is devoted to what he calls the "bounded neighborhood model" (1978: 155–56). Among the preliminary understandings essential to the discussion of tipping that follows is this: "Instead of everyone defining his neighborhood by reference to his own location, there is a common definition of the neighborhood and its boundaries. A person is either inside or outside" (Schelling 1978: 155). As Schelling recognizes, the sine qua non of the decision process upon which he builds his model, the very first datum that is required by the decision-maker, is the unambiguous definition of the spatial unit provided by a boundary.

Schelling deals with boundedness by stipulation, but this stipulation is not as innocuous as it might at first seem. There is considerable evidence that "a common definition of neighborhood" is in most cases lacking (Hunter 1975; Form et al. 1954; Molotch 1972; Haeberle 1988). Molotch (1972) demonstrates considerable disagreement among residents over the actual boundaries of South Shore (Chicago), and Hunter (1975) shows that neighborhood is actually a very plastic concept.

Despite their strengths, then, tipping models leave unanswered a critical question for understanding the creation of demographically and socioeconomically distinct suburbs. Like public choice theories, they are predicated upon the acquisition of information by individuals attempting to satisfy preferences through residential choice; but they do not tell us how that information is provided or how it may be structured.

### Hirschman: The Location Decisions of Connoisseurs

One thing that we can say unambiguously about persons moving to new residential or business locations is that they are simultaneously leaving old ones. This may seem a trivial observation, but Albert O. Hirschman has produced a provocative study of exit behavior (Hirschman 1970). His analysis of the dynamics of exit, in fact, has a great deal to offer with regard to understanding urban fragmentation.

An individual that is dissatisfied with an organization may resort to voice, relying on his status as a member of the organization to give weight to attempts at reform; or, he may exit in favor of some alternative organization that more nearly meets his expectations; or he may simply abide, demonstrating loyalty to the organization on the assumption that things will improve. Hirschman explores these behaviors in the context of a concern for organizational lapses that cause a deterioration in the quality of the product. One of the principal questions he poses is "when will such a deterioration provoke the exercise of voice and when will it result in exit?"

Confronting this question leads Hirschman to a perverse conclusion—deteriorating product quality is most likely to drive out the very consumers that might most effectively exercise the voice option (chapter 5). This is so because of the differing demand functions of two groups of consumers. When product price increases, the marginal consumer—the individual with limited resources—is first to exit. But when product quality deteriorates, the first

deserters are the connoissuers, the consumers who are interested above all in quality and are relatively unaffected
by fluctuations in price. These are precisely the individuals that would be most effective in pressing for recuperation. It is just because they are most concerned, however,
that they are most offended by declining quality and consequently are likely to be the first to exit.

The likelihood that the connoisseur will exercise one
option rather than the other depends upon the availability of alternatives of a quality higher than the original
product in its deteriorated state. Frequently, Hirshman
says, introducing a little competition into a monopoly situation produces undesirable outcomes (chapter 5). In the
case that the monopoly is flaccid (quite likely) and produces a low quality product, the connoisseurs will be
driven into the arms of the competitors. The remaining
clientele, with too few resources to exit in search of higher
quality, is not likely to be effective in invoking the voice
option. The result is a quasi-monopoly which can be expected to operate in a perpetual state of deterioration.

The dynamic that Hirschman sketches is valuable for
the insight that it provides into the contemporary urban
predicament. It is clearly compatible with the recent decline of central cities. The role of the connoisseur is played
by the middle-class white. The product he consumes is the
quality of life produced in political units. Because he typically has a surplus of resources to commit, his overriding
concern is with the "quality" of his quality of life rather
than the price he has to pay to obtain it. When he per-
ceives that the quality of life is deteriorating in central
cities—increasing crime, deteriorating schools, status
challenges from minority groups, crowding and air pollu-
tion—his preoccupation with this quality and his capacity
for absorbing the costs of relocation make him a prime
candidate for early exit. Furthermore, this potential for
exit can be readily realized since suburban communities
offer so many high quality alternatives to the central city.

The perniciousness of the dominance of exit over voice
in this case is that eventually central city populations are

created that are dependent upon city institutions—they can exercise neither exit nor voice. The central city continues to wallow along like Hirschman's Nigerian railway, producing sub-par outputs for consumers that have no choice but to accept them. At this stage deterioration is pathological, recuperation doubtful.

There is a further virtue in the analytical framework constructed by Hirschman. It permits us to think of the recruitment process as a complement to exclusion in the sorting dynamic that is perpetually in progress in metropolitan areas. Indeed, it combines the intuitions of the exclusionists and the political economists by distinguishing between the marginal consumer and the connoisseur. The connoisseur is the individual open to recruitment, sensitive to variations in life style, service delivery, and taxes. For the marginal consumer, accoutrements are largely irrelevant in the face of considerations of housing cost, daily cost of transportation to and from work, and so on. The marginal consumer is more likely to arrive at his eventual location by a process of exclusion rather than recruitment. The connoisseur fits more readily Tiebout's model of the perapatetic consumer, making his choices and voting with his feet.

## Overlooking the Obvious:
## The Implied Importance of Political Boundaries

Urban political boundaries are frequently cited as elements structuring urban spatial segregation in the literature of urban fragmentation. Williams, for instance, states:

> Our diverse research efforts, however, shared a common perception of basic urban processes. We assumed that metropolitan areas represent a set of political boundaries (central cities, smaller municipalities, counties, etc.) normally subject to a more or less continuous procession of people and jobs entering and leaving (B. Williams 1973).

Similarly, Skogan notes: "While earlier social stratification and geographic segregation by race, class, and culture were neighborhood level processes, the massive flight of the white middle class beyond the jurisdictional grasp of the schools, courts, police, and governments of many central cities has turned city boundaries into the relevant lines of cleavage" (Skogan 1977). And Dye and associates write: "To the political scientist, one of the most interesting attributes of metropolitan areas is the fact that urban specialization very often coincides with political boundaries" (1971).

Also of interest are remarks in the urban fragmentation literature that reveal the fundamental importance of "boundedness" and "bounding" for structuring human consciousness and behavior. Boundedness, for instance, is the essence of the concept of the natural area and the ecological understanding of neighborhood pioneered by Burgess, Park, and Mackenzie. The fact of boundedness was as important in their conceptualization for identifying the community and neighborhood as was the shared consciousness of residents. Hence, boundaries themselves were taken by them to be causal in the creation of sociologically distinct neighborhoods.

> Sociologists have discovered that every natural area is, or tends to become, in the natural course of events, a cultural area. Every natural area has, or tends to have, its own peculiar traditions, customs, conventions, standards of decency and propriety, and, if not a language of its own, at least a universe of discourse, in which words and acts have a meaning which is appreciably different for each local community (Park 1952b: 201).

Molotch, in his study of South Shore, discusses several aspects of the boundedness of the community (pp. 45–62). He notes the important consequences of the perception, or lack thereof, of boundedness and inclusiveness on the part of residents of an area for the demographic dynamics of that area.

> The exact location of South Shore's boundaries, the degree to which they are agreed upon, and the significance to residents of the territory they enclose, are of special importance in an area experiencing racial change. People's response to racial change can be reasonably expected to be dependent upon whether they place themselves within the boundaries of that changing community. It must be their community that is changing if they are to act (either as individuals or in unison) in response to the change (Molotch 1972: 45).

In South Shore, however, there was little agreement on the southern boundary of the community (pp. 45–50). Claims were made for a number of streets—83rd, 79th, 75th, 87th. Much of South Shore considered the southern area, Bradwell, to be a part of the community. The ambiguity of the southern boundary, however, permitted residents of Bradwell to consider themselves outside of South Shore and unaffected by its problems of racial change.

> Regardless of the net effect which the Bradwell problem had upon South Shore's racial composition, it is noteworthy that the behavior of Bradwell's residents can be explained in part by the boundary characteristics of the area in which they lived. The larger point is that the processes by which people determine boundaries to differentiate their geographical world are also processes which have consequences for community racial change (Molotch 1972: 61–62).

Lyons and Lowery (1986) discuss the importance of the "organization of political space" for various types of citizen participation and involvement in local government and the local community. They explore the implications of correspondence of jurisdictional boundaries with "social worlds"—spatial units in which " 'families with similar resources, beliefs, and habits' tend to cluster" (Lyons and Lowery, 1986: 322–23)—for the exercise of exit, voice, loyalty and neglect behaviors. These concerns are further pursued in a later piece (Lowery and Lyons 1989) which examines the "impact of jurisdictional boundaries" on the moving intentions of individuals.

The theoretical importance of boundaries for tipping-point theorists has been discussed, and they are clearly important for the public choice school also since it is boundaries which unite a particular bundle of goods, services, and taxes with a determinate place. Boundaries are of evident importance for urban analysts such as Stein (1987) who, following Tiebout, attempt to correlate differences in service cost and provision with population differences, and who find that indices of segregation are higher in MSAs which have higher numbers of suburban jurisdictions. Boundaries are similarly implicated in Logan and Schneider's (1981) analysis, in which they find income inequality among suburbs to have increased in SMSAs with high political fragmentation.

## Conclusion

There is little doubt that American metropolitan areas are highly fragmented. Much evidence indicates that jurisdictional fragmentation is paralleled by the spatial differentiation of racial, ethnic, and socioeconomic groups. This differentiation can be partially explained by invoking exclusionary powers; but exclusion alone cannot account for the persistence of white, middle class communities in the face of the high residential mobility and rapid population turnover that characterizes modern urban areas. A complete understanding of socio-spatial differentiation requires a theory of recruitment as a complement to exclusion. Treatments of recruitment tend to talk about motives—preferences for services or social and racial antipathies—that propel the recruitment dynamic without specifically discussing how individuals identify places that are compatible with their preferences. That is to say, they assume that individuals have the information that is prerequisite to acting upon their preferences (Tiebout 1956; Schelling 1978). This approach to the information component of the recruitment dynamic is overly casual in light of the fact that the type of information available to settlers and the way it is provided may well condition patterns of the distribution of persons and resources and, through them, a number of urban outcomes.

Social scientists of all sorts, either in their explicit remarks or by what is implicit in the assumptions they make in their analyses, point to urban political boundaries as elements structuring the process in which persons and resources are distributed across spatial units. Given these fairly clear references, formal boundaries are characterized by a surprising invisibility. We know that they are there, but we don't see them. They are the least ambiguous aspect of urban political fragmentation—that, in fact, may be the reason that they are taken so much for granted. For there is no analysis of urban political boundaries as such. It is frequently assumed that they are sorting mechanisms, but no attention is given to determining how, exactly, they sort. Nor is any consideration given to the comparative effectiveness of urban political boundaries and other types of sorting mechanisms—neighborhood boundaries, for example. There has been no consideration of the conditions under which boundaries sort most effectively, nor any attempt to determine which boundaries are the best sorters. Finally, there has been little appreciation that some of the sorting attributed to direct action on the part of institutions and individuals may in fact be produced passively by the system of political boundaries.

The examination of the literature of urban fragmentation in this chapter, then, inspires two observations. One is that a better understanding of urban residential recruitment is needed, particularly as it is dependent upon the provision of information to persons with preferences that are making locational decisions. A second is that, though urban political boundaries are widely cited by social scientists concerned with various problems and curiosities of the fragmented metropolis, little has been done to understand the workings of boundaries themselves. It is to a theoretical statement of the role of suburban political boundaries in structuring information used by persons making locational decisions that this study turns in chapter 2.

# 2

## Place, Preferences, and Information: Political Boundaries and Population Sorting

In 1973, Brian J. L. Berry wrote of the creation of a "mosaic culture" in the metropolitan areas of the United States. Changes in transportation and communications technologies had permitted population expansion at the urban periphery. These same developments heralded new possibilities for households making locational decisions. In an era in which the city had been replaced by the "daily urban system," such households could survey whole metropolitan geographies, North to South, East to West, choosing from the entire panoply of possibilities the location that most nearly matched their preferences regarding life style, consumption patterns, prestige, and so on. One of the human consequences of urbanization was a culture in which social differences took on geographical manifestations—in which geographic compartments existed, perhaps were created, expressly to mirror the life style preferences of particular narrowly defined groups. Each of these compartments was like a tile in a mosaic—discrete, distinctive in color, separate from the other compartments.

31

The results of other analyses appear to give some credence to Berry's conceptualization. Most metropolitan areas in the United States are highly segregated by race (Duncan and Duncan 1957; Sorenson, Taeuber, and Hollingsworth 1974; Van Valey, Roof, and Wilcox 1977). Levels of segregation have not been reduced, even by federal court orders and civil rights legislation in the fifties and sixties (Massey and Denton 1987). Considerable barriers to black suburbanization still exist (Massey and Denton 1987, 1988a), and blacks living in the suburbs are confined to older communities close to central cities (Stahura 1988; R. Farley 1970; Logan and Schneider 1984).

Compartmentalization in metropolitan areas is most complete by race, but the mosaic includes socioeconomic compartmentalization as well. Studies have found increasing income differences among suburban jurisdictions (Miller 1981; Logan and Schneider 1981). One recent study (Stein 1987) reports that segregation by race, education, income, and age increases with the number of municipal governments in a metropolitan area (though only the coefficient for education is significant at 0.05 level).

What are the causes of the rise of the mosaic culture? Berry describes the broad technological and macrosocial developments that make possible the creation of daily urban systems, but what are the "micromotives" that underly "macrobehavior" (Schelling 1978)? As Berry's reference to highly mobile households seeking suitable locations would indicate, these broad patterns of segregation and compartmentalization must ultimately be accretions of individual decisions.

This chapter attempts to isolate the basic elements of decision for settlers, individuals engaged in housing search. It first presents a discussion of the political geography of metropolitan areas, and the importance of political boundaries in the definition of places. The preferences of settlers, and the information that is required if they are to attempt to satisfy their preferences, are then discussed. The crux of location search is the interaction among place, information, and preferences. This interaction is likely to be stronger when the definition of place is more precise and complete. Factors affecting the definition of place are discussed, as well as the causal impact of political boundaries on population sorting. Finally, the implications of resource differences among settlers for sorting dynamics, and for life chances in metropolitan areas are discussed.

## Political Boundaries and the Definition of Place

There has been a good deal of discussion of urban fragmentation and its implications, particularly for questions of equality and efficiency (Danielson 1976; Orfield 1978; Tiebout 1956; V. Ostrom, Tiebout, and Warren 1970; Miller 1981; E. Ostrom 1983, 1980; Bish 1971; Cion 1971). The parties to this discussion, however, seldom recognize that their common referent is, at base, a system of political boundaries. The urban fragmentation literature tends to understand differences in jurisdictions in racial, ethnic, socioeconomic, and economic terms without remembering that all of these differences grow out of an elementary geographic fact—that one place is not another—and that this fact of geography is frequently given formal status in the drawing of boundaries.

The strategy of this study, then, is to approach urban jurisdictional fragmentation beginning with the fundamental datum that urban areas are spatially subdivided by formal boundaries. This is the least ambiguous aspect of urban political fragmentation. These boundaries perform a number of functions.

The first function of boundaries is geographic. They demarcate discrete parcels of land. The differences between sub-units in urban areas are first understood by understanding that they are different places.

If the matter were to end with geography, there would be little to inspire comment. It is because geographic boundaries incorporate a number of other functions that they are interesting. The most obvious among these is the political function. Boundaries in urban areas wed geographic expanses to political authority. Hence municipalities, for instance, are not only places but public agencies with certain legal powers and responsibilities— the power to tax, the power to spend, power over land use, the responsibility to provide services, and so on. The political boundary is a compound symbol of political authority exercised in a finite geographic area.

Political boundaries also perform economic functions. Geographic and economic functions interact because firms are typically located in discrete places. A number of economic effects—employment (Kasarda 1985, 1983), the distribution of goods and services—are mediated by geographic factors. The political, economic, and geographic functions interact because political units generally exercise a monopoly over certain sources of tax revenue within their jurisdiction. Hence, the number and nature of firms located within a boundary greatly affects the types and levels of public services that political units are able to provide. In turn, the policies adopted by political units and imposed in particular places influence the location decisions of firms (Schneider 1985).

Finally, political boundaries perform social functions. They define populations, and, as with politics and economics, they structure the interaction of population and geography. Political boundaries become identified with the people who live within them. These people may be socioeconomically, racially, enthnically, religiously, or culturally distinctive. The existence of a boundary gives this social distinctiveness a geographic component. The identity of the population in such a specifically defined place is not only religious, cultural, racial or ethnic, but geographic as well. The individuals which comprise such a population are, among other things, the people that live in *that* place.

In effect, this is a study of the meaning of "place." It conceives of a place in a metropolitan area not merely as a geographic entity, but as an intersection of political factors, economics, and social characteristics with geography. A place is an amalgam of all of these components.

A formal political boundary defines the geographic component of place more precisely, but in so doing, because geography interacts with other dimensions, it necessarily makes its social and economic identity more clear, and it simultaneously creates political identity. A formal boundary makes a place more socially, economically, and politically distinctive as well as more geographically distinctive.

By sharpening (if not in some cases creating) the sense of place, political boundaries support sorting among individuals who have definite preferences about the places in which they live, learn, and perhaps work.

## The Location Decision: Preferences and Information

In this book, the assumption is that households and individuals who are moving are attempting to satisfy certain preferences. Indeed, a move may be an express attempt to find a location more in conformity with the movers' preferences; but even if it is undertaken of necessity because of a transfer or change in the life-cycle, the mover will be attempting to find a location that satisfies certain wants. These preferences are likely to concern the quality of housing, the quality of certain publicly provided services, the life style likely to predominate in a new location, and the socioeconomic status, race, ethnicity, and nationality of neighbors.

This assumption has a certain affinity with the preoccupations of the rational choice paradigm in economics and political science. Rational choice assumptions and methods can be fruitfully applied to the choice problem that faces individuals making location decisions. Rational choice analyses have been most productive in substantive areas, such as voting and legislative behavior, where the structure of choice problems permits analysts to anticipate the roles that decision-makers will assume, and thus the preferences they are likely to have, as well as the constraints they are likely to face in attempting to satisfy their preferences. Downs (1957: 4–8), for instance, judges the rationality of the actions of voters, politicians, and political parties only with respect to the goals that can reasonably be imputed to these actors *as* voters, politicians, and political parties. Such actors may have (indeed, inevitably will have) goals as persons aside from their goals in these roles, but to consider every possible goal causes the analysis to degenerate into tautology, settling into the comfortable posture that, ultimately, folks do what they want and want whatever it is they do (Downs 1957: 6). The choice context of housing search permits the definition of roles, suggests certain goals that can be imputed to persons filling those roles, and includes fairly predictable constraints facing such persons. The use of these elements facilitates the development of theoretical considerations that inform this study.

This is where the common ground between this study and rational choice studies ends, however. Rational choice methods are not used in this study. It is more concerned with explaining the macro-social patterns that result from micro-decisions than with the decision process itself. There are no formal models of decision-making in this book, nor proofs that particular decision outcomes follow from a particular structure of preferences and constraints.

## The Nature of Household Preferences for Locations

By concentrating on the preferences of settlers, this study is only making explicit an implied concern of much of the work previously discussed (Schelling 1978; Tiebout 1956; E. Ostrom 1983; V. Ostrom Tiebout and Warren 1970; Berry 1973; Peterson 1981; Stein 1987; Danielson 1976; Lyons and Lowery 1986; Lowery and Lyons 1989). These preferences are likely to be intensely felt. They are rooted deeply in the concerns that have traditionally revolved around family and domestic life.

Gerald Suttles (1972) identifies a number of the psychological and social functions that the neighborhood (what we here would rather conceive of as a "generic residential space") performs for its residents, and, in turn, the sorts of things that settlers are likely to seek in their neighborhoods. Neighborhoods reduce uncertainty about neighbors, permitting one to anticipate the sorts of social situations which are likely to arise, the probable actions of neighbors toward oneself and the nature of appropriate reactions. Neighborhood reduces threats of all kinds, reduces social tension between groups and individuals, lessens the possibility of challenges from other social groups. In their residential spaces, individuals seek shared cultural understandings about family, work, relationships among individuals of different sexes and diverse age groups, the nature and possession of property, the rearing of children, the scope of autonomy and privacy to be accorded one's fellows. Outside of the home, the residential space stands as the next bulwark against all sorts of alien influences, a sort of security perimeter. The neighborhood is a means of exerting control over chaotic forces which, in the more remote world, may be irresistable.

> The scale of urban regions has brought complexity and the rapidity of urban change produces uncertainty and insecurity. The whole is too large for the individual to comprehend. In the search for self-identity in a mass society, he seeks to minimize disorder by living in a neighbourhood in which life is comprehensible and social relations predictable. Indeed, he moves out of 'his' neighborhood when he can no longer predict the consequences of a particular pattern of behaviour. He seeks an enclave of relative homogeneity: a predictable life style; a territory free from status competition because his neighbours are 'just like him'; a turf compatible in outlook because his neighbours are at similar stages in the life cycle; a safe area, free from status-challenging ethnic or racial minorities; a haven from complexity, to be protected and safeguarded by whatever means—legal, institutional, and frequently illegal violence, each a symptom of defensive territoriality protecting that which has been achieved (Berry 1973).

Elijah Anderson (1985) describes the unusual sociology and the sorts of adjustments residents have to make

in an inner city neighborhood which is racially and socioeconomically complex and therefore offers none of the sim-
plifying features that are usually present for households
and individuals in their residential spaces. The social and
racial heterogeneity of neighbors makes them unpredict-
able in the eyes of the residents of this neighborhood, and
an occasional mugging or assault reinforces this impression. Consequently, the daily routines of residents include
specific pathways and routes which minimize threat, elab-
orate street etiquettes devised to avoid confrontation, and
mental note-taking meant to familiarize the individual
with potentially dangerous persons, locations, situations.
A principal concern of residents is security and, in particular, being able to navigate the streets safely. Young people, particularly young black males, who might in other
circumstances not merit a second glance, are scrutinized
as potential attackers. Anderson describes

> a peculiar and very local code of street etiquette—[the
> neighborhood's] own system of behavioral prescriptions
> and proscriptions for handling others on the streets
> with a minimum of trouble. Such a code might well be
> viewed as a collective response to the common problems
> local people face each time they venture into the streets.
> How much eye contact to give or allow from what sort of
> person on what streets at what time of day, whom to
> talk with and what to say, where not to walk the dog,
> how to stand at the corner, the safest though quite indi-
> rect route to one's destination, how to carry one's pock-
> etbook, how much money to carry (in case of a
> mugging), or the appropriate way to behave in a stickup
> situation all have their place in the street code of the
> village (Anderson 1985: 121).

Previous research has indicated that there are not
many stably integrated areas in the United States, and
Anderson's analysis, coupled with the understanding of
neighborhood developed by Suttles, Berry, Lauman (1966),
and others, demonstrate why. The residential space is precisely the context in which people are *least* able to tolerate diversity. At work, at large in the city, shopping in a

commercial area, individuals expect and tolerate diversity in racial characteristics, manifestations of socioeconomic status, public behavior. In the area around the home, however, most people seek certainty and security. Few are willing to make the extensive adaptations and expose themselves to the uncertainty that Anderson recounts.

These comments indicate the nature of residential space and the preferences individuals are likely to have about such places. In general, given the desire of settlers to reduce tension, threat, challenge, they will seek out places where the inhabitants are likely to be like themselves in external characteristics. Whether or not it is justified, most people take external characteristics such as race and the external manifestations of socioeconomic status to be indications of probable behavior, moral character, and attitudes. One reason that such characteristics are employed as cues is that they are accessible. To go more deeply into the matter of identification and ascription imposes costs in the form of time, and possibly personal injury.

Danielson (1976: chapter 1) notes the influence that differences of race, ethnicity, and class have on the geographic dispersion of social groups. Whites continue to identify blacks with "poverty, crime, broken families, and other undesirable characteristics of lower-class populations" (Danielson 1976: 11). A primary motivation of middle class households in their search for suitable residences is to avoid exposure to minority and low socioeconomic status households. This motivation is based on considerations of social status and prestige as well as concern for security (Berry 1973; McClelland 1961). Residence and neighborhood are important physical indications of success in a materially oriented society.

The extent to which white, middle class households are averse to residential contact with the minority poor is revealed in broad patterns of white flight from central cities. The motivations which culminate in a move by a particular household are complex, but most studies indicate that where blacks are present in significant number, avoidance of black residential concentration explains some part of the moving decision (Frey 1979; Marshall 1979).

In order to achieve some correspondence between preferences and objective conditions in particular places, settlers require information. Information about places enables individuals making locational decisions to search for suitable locations in a purposeful, rational manner. If information about places is available, settlers can hope that their efforts may be successful. In the absence of such information, housing search becomes a futile endeavor.

The search for an appropriate location can be understood as an attempt to define "distinct subareas, each of which is relatively homogeneous with respect to the chance of finding an acceptable vacancy" (Smith and Clark 1980). Success in such an effort first requires a means of identifying discrete places which can be distinguished from one another. Secondly, it requires the gathering of information about such places so that those which are clearly unsuitable can be screened out in summary fashion, and those which are "relatively homogeneous with respect to the chance of finding an acceptable vacancy" can be investigated further.

In the process of identifying places, filtering out the majority, and inspecting others more closely, settlers are likely to possess limited resources and to face heavy information costs. Particularly when they are moving from outside of the metropolitan area, it is doubtful that they will have unlimited time to make their decision. Trips to the new city to look at housing, and possibly schools, are expensive. Metropolitan housing markets are large and diverse. Settlers are likely to focus on that information which is most accessible and least ambiguous, information which offers some combination of the virtues of being uncostly and reliable.

## Political Boundaries and Information

The overriding theoretical preoccupation of this book is that formal political boundaries provide a basis for thinking of places as different from one another, the first step in acquiring information about places. This frame of reference is easily accessible to the settler—s/he can buy a map of the metropolitan area from most service stations and convenience stores, for instance. Such a frame of reference can readily be converted into a cognitive map as a prelude to the process of identifying and inspecting relatively homoeneous sub-units which promise to contain suitable locations. The system of political boundaries in a metropolitan area facilitates the process in which persons who are guided by certain preferences form expectations about those preferences being satisfied in one place or another. In sum, political boundaries provide the structure which is prerequisite to the generation of information that movers need, and they play a role in conveying that information to them. One empirical expectation, given this structure of information, would be that population sorting on socioeconomic, racial, and ethnic characteristics would be supported by political boundaries; and that political boundaries should become racial, social, and economic boundaries as well.

A critical property of boundaries in creating such a frame of reference is the clarity which they add to the definition of place. Schelling argues that a prerequisite to the population sorting which he examines in his bounded neighborhood model is that "there is a common definition of the neighborhood and its boundaries—a person is either inside or outside" (Schelling 1978: 155). It is precisely because political boundaries create such a common definition that they are worthy of attention. In the suburbs of metropolitan areas, political boundaries in fact create "bounded neighborhoods".

Municipal and school district boundaries create discrete residential spaces with near absolute precision. There is no ambiguity about the spatial dimension of such places. Within the perimeter of the city of Houston, Texas, there might be some question about the exact geographic identity of prestigious neighborhoods such as River Oaks and Memorial, but there is no question about the location of West University, Bunker Hill, or Piney Point because these latter communities are incorporated. A person buying a house at the periphery of River Oaks may claim to live in that neighborhood—his realtor will almost certainly give assurances of that fact—but others, more centrally located in that neighborhood may deny the claim, and the invitation to join the civic club may never come. Such a dispute cannot be authoritatively settled, because there are competing claims to authority when neighborhood boundaries are in question. The point is not in question with respect to West University, however, because in addition to being a neighborhood, it is a political jurisdiction. Political officials determine the outcome of any boundary dispute with authority and certainty. Indeed, the presence of a political boundary defining West University is probably one of the factors that has made it so attractive to the upper middle class.

## Formal Boundaries v. Informal Boundaries

A discussion of city neighborhoods and their informal boundaries should display the critical characteristics of political boundaries in greater relief. The problem that neighborhood boundaries present to settlers with specific preferences about locations is that they blur the geographic component of place, making it difficult to compare preferences and objective conditions. The first information requirement of settlers, the existence of discrete spatial units from which to choose, is incompletely satisfied by informal neighborhood boundaries.

It would be pointless to deny that spatial relationships reflect social relationships within large cities as well as across jurisdictional boundaries. A long tradition of urban ecological research stands as testimony to the fact that geographic areas within cities tend to become socioeconomically and culturally distinct and to maintain that distinctiveness over time (Park 1952b, 1952c). Park, Burgess, and Mackenzie, and their students have argued that "natural areas" tend to be populated by "natural groups" that differ from each other by race, age group, occupation, ethnicity, religion, family structure, and so on (Park 1952c: 170, 172).

This argument is apparently confirmed by subsequent research that reveals that large cities are characterized by substantial occupational segregation (Feldman and Tilly 1966; Duncan and Duncan 1955a). Other research indicates that spatially identifiable populations exhibit distinct behaviors as well. A large literature demonstrates that crime has a marked spatial component (Schmid 1960a, 1960b; Shaw and Mckay 1969; Harries 1974; Harries and Georges-Abeyie 1980; Voss and Peterson 1971; Kohfeld and Sprague 1988). The linkage between socioeconomic characteristics and spatial relationships even appears to have implications for the ways in which cities grow (Burgess 1925; Hoyt 1939). Much research uses factor analysis to demonstrate that areas of cities can be differentially characterized with regard to clusters of social, economic, and demographic variables (Hunter 1975; Schmid 1960a; Shevky and Bell 1955; Shevky and Williams 1949).

Most subsequent research, however, casts serious doubt upon the validity of the natural area concept. Frequently, the natural area defined by the researcher does not occur so naturally in the cognitive maps of its residents. Hunter (1975) found that the names and boundaries of the natural areas in Chicago identified by Burgess were not widely recognized fifty years later. Even in cases where the name was used by residents (about 40%) there was little agreement on boundaries. A substantial number of persons could supply no name or boundary for their neighborhood, and many areas had acquired new names and perceptions of boundaries had changed.

Indeed, Hunter found that the individual's conception of community tends to be functionally derived. It depends upon the class, age, family status, race, and other characteristics of the conceiver, as well as his primary group relationships and the spatial distinctiveness of areas. Thus, the relevant community for one individual may be the "social block"; for another, it may be an entire region (Hunter

1975: 112–114). These findings are echoed by Form and associates: ". . . different indices of social integration and intimacy had different territorial distributions. Some of them pointed to integration at the neighborhood level, some to the sub-community, and others to the city as a whole" (Form et al. 1954: 436).

Furthermore, the areas that much of this literature speaks of frequently are ambiguously or inconsistently delimited. In some cases, they are census tracts which might or might not correspond to anything that residents would recognize as a neighborhood (Form et al. 1954). In some cases, they are arbitrarily defined concentric zones or sectors that are convenient for the purposes of the researcher but appear nowhere outside of his research design (Schmid 1960b; Duncan and Duncan 1955a). Or they may be "commonly recognized" areas of the city (Schmid 1960a, 1960b), though the extent to which they are commonly recognized by residents is not demonstrated. Finally, the theoretical and cognitive implications of loading on certain factors by area are often unclear. Frequently, spatial distinctiveness with regard to a particular cluster of variables is not explained in terms of a social theory that demonstrates the causes of this distinctiveness and its impact on the behavior in question. Nor is it obvious that distinctiveness on one or more of these dimensions impinges on the awareness of residents of the city.

In short, though it is universally recognized that there are distinctive neighborhoods in cities, their precise names, boundaries, and socioeconomic characters are not easily determined. Frequently, such areas are not recognized by people who have lived in them for years (Hunter 1975). Locating such neighborhoods with any precision and characterizing them with respect to amenities, style of life, socioeconomic and racial composition of the population must be problematic for movers whose familiarity with local housing markets may be relatively slight.

In comparison to the informal boundaries which define, in loose fashion, neighborhoods, political boundaries are much more precise and more readily accessible. Place identity tends to be unambiguous only at some central point which everyone recognizes as within the neighborhood, while place identity is uniform for political jurisdictions from the center to the very periphery. Political boundaries, then, are more visible than neighborhood boundaries, and information about politically defined residential spaces is likely to be acquired at less cost than information about neighborhoods.

Additionally, judicial decisions and public policy over the last thirty-five years may well have increased the salience of political boundaries relative to informal neighborhood boundaries. (These judicial decisions and federal policies are discussed in greater detail in chapter 4.) Such policy developments have eliminated many neighborhood level discriminatory mechanisms such as restrictive covenants and segregated attendance zones within school districts. At the same time, discriminatory arrangements which work across jurisdictional boundaries, such as land use controls, have been reaffirmed in the federal courts in a series of opinions (chapter 4). The summary impact of this historical pattern in public policy should be to increase the importance of political boundaries for settlers whose preference is for homogeneous residential areas. School district and municipal boundaries may therefore constitute the last remaining bastion for those who wish to isolate themselves in communities and schools with "their own kind".

This shift toward increased salience of formal boundaries is probably most apparent in education. An increasingly important educational issue has been the imposition of interdistrict remedies to accomplish the integration of majority black central city school systems (for instance, *Milliken v. Bradley*, 1974; *Liddell v. St. Louis Board of Education*, 1972; *Brinkman v. Dayton Board of Education*, 1979; *Columbus Board of Education v. Penick*, 1979; *Evans v. Buchanan*, 1980; see also, in housing, *Hills v. Gautreaux*, 1975; see Orfield 1978: 30–36; Dimond 1985).

This comparison of formal political boundaries and informal neighborhood boundaries implies that segregation by race and class should be greater among jurisdictions than among neighborhoods. Such an implication can be evaluated at two levels.

First, segregation among neighborhoods and among municipalities can be compared for suburban municipalities (this is the strategy pursued in chapter 4 of this book). If segregation across municipalities is greater than segregation within municipalities, there is reason to believe that the argument is correct—that political boundaries provide less costly information than neighborhood boundaries, and hence population sorting by characteristics salient for the preferences of settlers is more efficient at municipal boundaries than at neighborhood boundaries. The result of other analyses are suggestive here. Miller (1981) finds increasing class differentiation by municipality in Los Angeles County; and Logan and Schneider (1981) obtain similar results for 31 of 51 large metropolitan areas. This question is pursued in chapter 4 where it is found that most of the variance in class and racial composition of suburban populations in Cook County, Illinois, and Los Angeles County occurs across municipalities rather than within them.

Second, levels of segregation among suburban municipalities can be compared with levels of segregation among neighborhoods in central cities. A similar analysis has already been done (Massey and Denton 1988a). The authors find that blacks are more highly segregated in central cities than in suburbs. They urge caution in interpreting these results, however. Though black segregation levels are higher in central cities on average, segregation levels in the suburbs are still quite high (Massey and Denton 1988a: 605). Low levels of black suburban segregation tend to be found in metropolitan areas with few blacks.

Furthermore, this analysis does not address the argument made here, since the spatial unit used for computing segregation indices in both the central cities and suburbs is the census tract. The argument in this book calls for segregation by municipality in the suburbs to be compared with segregation by neighborhood in the central cities, and there are no studies that make precisely this comparison. It should be noted in passing that a number of studies suggest that segregation by race and class is increasing among suburban municipalities, while the exodus of the middle class from central cities makes them more socially homogeneous.

## Political Boundary Configuration

One property of boundaries that might be expected to influence the effectiveness with which they sort demographic and socioeconomic groups is their relationship to one another. Do the boundaries of various jurisdictions coincide or are they cross-cutting? Are the jurisdictions coterminous, or do they overlap? When the boundaries of jurisdictions, particularly municipalities and school districts, coincide, the layering of functions on the boundary is increased, and the boundary becomes more salient for individuals making locational decisions. Orthogonal boundaries, however, make the relationship between political authority, public functions and services, and urban geography more diffuse and fractional. Other things being equal, one would expect that coinciding boundaries will be more effective in sorting on demographic and socioeconomic characteristics than cross-cutting boundaries.

Coinciding boundaries should sort more effectively because the layering of functions on a single political boundary reduces information costs to settlers. When the school district and the municipality are coterminous, for instance, information about the social characteristics of neighborhoods is also information about the characteristics of the social context of schools. One can safely assume that the student body to which one's child will be exposed will have the same socioeconomic status and religious, racial, and ethnic composition as the general population of the municipality. If the municipality is split between school districts or served by a district which extends far beyond municipal boundaries, acquiring information about schools becomes an additional and equal task to acquiring information about the residence. Under such circumstances, can one be sure that one's child will attend a school within the home community? Is the school district racially diverse? Do its boundaries contain large concentrations of minority children who attend schools inside the home community, or who go to schools which one's child must also attend? Will children have to be bused to schools a very long way from home? If the boundaries of municipality and school district are identical, additional questions such as these do not arise. Information is less costly than the case in which boundaries are orthogonal.

The problem created by cross-cutting boundaries is that they cause settlers to think of a location as falling within two places rather than one. There is the place in which one's associations with neighbors are determined; and there is the place in which one's children will go to school. When boundaries coincide, the places are the same. When boundaries are orthogonal, these places differ. They are not the same geographically, and the difference in geography raises the possibility of other differences, other outcomes which have implications for distinct sets of preferences. Cross-cutting boundaries blur the sense of place and complicate the decision process.

It is reasonable to expect that individuals making locational decisions are likely to filter out alternatives for which cues are ambiguous, and which present additional information costs before a final decision based on overriding preferences can be made. They should expend their resources where they are likely to offer the greatest and most immediate return, which is to say that they will look further into alternatives which repay their efforts with reliable information, and are likely not to pursue alternatives about which initial efforts produce conflicting signals.

This general expectation should be clarified in two ways. First, this study argues that alternatives in overlapping jurisdictions may be rejected because information about these alternatives is more costly, *not* because these alternatives are less desirable. In fact, had the settler pursued the alternative which presented a case of cross-cutting boundaries, he may have found it to be perfectly suitable. Indeed, some number of individuals will persist in acquiring information about such alternatives, and will choose them over others in coterminous jurisdictions where information was more clearly structured and, hence, less costly.

This impinges upon the second point of clarification, which is that this discussion is not meant to pose dichotomous alternatives. Differences in suburban jurisdictional populations are produced by forces which do not operate as switches—they do not turn population flows on and off. Rather, they make small changes in probabilities, they increase or depress rates of influx and emigration. A jurisdictional population acquires some eccentricity of socioeconomic or demographic character, or exchanges one eccentricity for another, gradually, over a period of years or decades. In order to produce eccentric populations, the forces and mechanisms which direct or deflect population flows need not erect absolute barriers. They need only assign a somewhat higher percentage of persons with a particular characteristic to one place, and a somewhat lower percentage to other places.

Therefore the argument is not, for instance, that a municipality which is split between school districts will attract no middle class households for which quality of educational services is an overriding concern. Indeed, there may be residences in that community that carry access to excellent educational programs, and some number of settlers for whom schools are important will seek those residences out. This study does argue, however, that other alternatives which can more easily be identified as offering excellent schools will attract more of such households. Those places should be eccentric (in this context, in terms of having a higher percentage of middle class households with school children) while places which present ambiguous cues, because they are defined by cross-cutting jurisdictional boundaries, should fall in the middling range of communities.

*Cross-cutting Boundaries: Empirical Expectations*

Empirically, when formal political boundaries are orthogonal, the populations residing within boundaries should be less distinctive in their characteristics than populations residing in areas where boundaries of various types coincide. Respecting several dimensions of population composition—race, ethnicity, and socioeconomic status—split jurisdictions should be relatively clustered about the mean values for their metropolitan areas, while unified jurisdictions should be more likely to fall toward the tails of the distributions. Consequently, an aggregate of split jurisdictions should be less segregated along these dimensions than an aggregate of unified jurisdictions. This result may arise from one of two patterns of settlement within the jurisdictions.

The first pattern, which might be called the "gray" pattern, is the straightforward result of the ambiguity of the cues that are presented to individuals making locational decisions. Ambiguous cues should produce jurisdictional populations that are not distinctive. In other words, such populations should not be unusually high or low in terms of median years of schooling completed, should not be unusually high or low in terms of mean income, should not be heavily black or entirely white, and so on.

This lack of distinctiveness is produced because a split jurisdiction is more apt to attract individuals and households in residual categories. These are people, perhaps, with no strong preferences about those considerations which are of intense concern to others. They may have concerns which, given their objective racial and socioeconomic status, are idiosyncratic. They may settle in a place to be close to a job or a facility of a particular type such as a hospital or a shopping mall. They may be individuals for whom architectural and historical interest may be the most important properties of housing, making neighborhood quality, services, and characteristics of neighbors less important in their decision calculus. Split jurisdictions provide ambiguous cues about those characteristics and conditions which are traditionally most salient to persons engaged in housing search, and consequently they are less likely to attract such persons. Long term sorting processes, then, should result in more individuals and households in these residual categories being shunted into split jurisdictions and into locations for which more traditional settlers do not compete as intensely.

The result should be a jurisdiction which is nearly "average" in terms of the composition of its population, and which is not highly segregated internally. The internal distribution of population over geography should be relatively neutral, with no areas within the jurisdiction showing extreme concentrations of any racial, ethnic, or socioeconomic group. Furthermore, if a group of such jurisdictions were examined to determine the aggregate level of segregation among jurisdictions, the level should be low compared to unified jurisdictions in the same metropolitan area.

The gray pattern of internal settlement of split jurisdictions, then, produces communities which are nondistinctive on the whole because the relative internal diversity of their populations is uniformly distributed geographically. However, such nondistinctiveness at the jurisdictional and aggregate level might also result if internal diversity were rigidly spatially structured. Such cases display a "black and white" pattern of internal settlement, rather than gray. Distinct areas within the jurisdictional boundary would be populated by individuals of one racial, ethnic, or socioeconomic group, while other distinct areas would be populated by individuals of different groups. Eighty-five percent of the jurisdiction might be entirely white, for instance, while fifteen percent might be completely black. Such a pattern of internal settlement would also produce jurisdictions which appear to be nondistinctive with respect to race, though at a lower level of aggregation, the black-and-white pattern is obviously quite different from the gray pattern.

Such a pattern may be produced when the boundary that crosses through a jurisdiction retains high visibility. The overall expectation is that cross-cutting boundaries confound information about functions, services, quality and style of life, and demographic and socioeconomic composition. One reason is that cross-cutting boundaries produce a crossing and confounding of functions rather than the layering of functions that typifies coinciding boundaries. In spite of this, it may be the case that a crossing boundary defines a jurisdiction which is so famous or infamous for the services it provides or the composition of its population that it retains high salience in spite of the potential inconsistency of cues that would be expected from such boundary relationships.

For example, a school district may have such a reputation for the quality of its academic programs and facilities that its boundary retains high salience no matter where it falls in relation to other boundaries. If the boundary of such a district splits a municipality, and the neighboring district has no such reputation, this boundary may broadly structure differences in socioeconomic status within the municipality. Middle class households may compete for locations within the more prestigious district, driving up their prices, and causing the exclusion of less favored households from the market. If the class composition of the population of such a municipality were examined, it would be found to be unremarkable, including considerable diversity among households in socioeconomic status. Closer examination, however, would reveal considerable homogeneity within geographic areas structured by the school district boundary.

Both the gray pattern and black-and-white pattern of internal jurisdictional settlement are plausible results of cross-cutting boundary systems. Both will appear similar at two levels of examination. That is, each will produce jurisdictions which, when grouped, will appear to be relatively unsegregated across jurisdictions. Also, each will produce jurisdictions which, when examined singly, will appear to fall in the middling range on salient dimensions of population composition. It is only when internal population variations are analyzed that the difference in patterns will emerge.

Whatever the specific internal pattern of settlement, however, cross-cutting jurisdictional boundaries should produce populations which are less distinctive overall than jurisdictional boundaries that coincide.

### The Causal Nature of Political Boundaries

Finally, the theory presented in this book asserts that political boundaries have a causal influence on population sorting and segregation by race and class. The intention to begin this consideration of urban outcomes not with a focus on institutional factors or on political officials, but on the system of political boundaries which is the irreducible foundation of metropolitan political fragmentation has repeatedly been declared. Such a beginning, it has been argued, could well lead to some of the outcomes that other studies explain by focusing on institutions, policies, and key political decision-makers. The claim has been made that differentiation among metropolitan populations must eventuate from recruitment and aggregation of favored groups as well as exclusion and segregation of disadvantaged groups.

At this point, I would like to offer a conjecture about the type of process in which political boundaries would play a causal role. This discussion will further illustrate some of the theoretical concerns and relationships among factors that inform this study.

One can imagine that at some point in an ideal past, all jurisdictions contained all types of people living harmoniously together. There was no spatial segregation, nor was there inequality by jurisdiction. Populations were not conscious of themselves as such. Political boundaries were in place, existing entirely for administrative convenience. In some cases, perhaps, the creation of boundaries preceded the actual settlement of an area in anticipation of population growth (see chapter 6 on the history of school districts in St. Louis County). In such a world, how might the sorting of populations by race and class begin?

In answering this question, one needs first to make an assumption about place identity and the way in which political boundaries convey information. It is assumed that it is only when the population of a jurisdiction has become noticeably different from the greater population that the boundaries of the jurisdiction begin to convey information. A nondistinctive jurisdiction has geographical definition and the rudimentary outlines of place, but it has no strong place identity. If a population is in all significant respects like the greater population in a metropolitan area, the boundaries that define it provide no strong cues to a person that wants to live among people that are similar to her in some regard. A settler that is committed to living among neighbors of similar education, occupational status, family and class background, and racial or ethnic identity will not be entirely repelled by such a place; neither will she be strongly attracted to it. In all likelihood, if it is considered at all, such a place will be screened out early in the individual's decision process. A community with no distinctive characteristics supports no strong messages at its boundaries. However, once a jurisdictional population is distinctive with regard to one or more salient characteristics, the boundaries that define it begin to provide settlers with a picture of how these characteristics are manifested over a particular geography. They then can make rational location decisions based upon preferences with regard to these characteristics.

Political boundaries in metropolitan areas are interesting because they facilitate the development of a sense of distinctive place. They do so initially by unambiguously distinguishing spatial units, units which are discrete, pristine, and exclusive. This is in fact the stage at which development has arrived in the ideal past that has been postulated. This stage is prerequisite to a rational attempt by an individual making location decisions to match preferences to objective conditions. But in such an ideal past, how would objective conditions begin to vary across spatial units?

This theory asserts that any jurisdiction will become eccentric with finite probability. This probability is greater for jurisdictions with compactly drawn boundaries rather than extended ones. Once eccentricity occurs in a jurisdictional population, culture, demography, and life style begin to interact with geography, the jurisdiction acquires an identity as a place, and the information that is structured and conveyed by political boundaries tends to perpetuate that identity.

All that is necessary to the argument that eccentricity will occur in jurisdictions is faith in probability. The number of persons moving through the central city of an urban area is a large sample of the total population. In the ideal past, for any salient characteristic, the proportion of the population of large political units bearing the characteristic approaches the proportional value of the entire area. On the other hand, the number of persons moving through a small, suburban jurisdiction may be a very small fraction of the total population. It is much easier for the distribution of some characteristic over a small population to become skewed with respect to the overall distribution of that characteristic. Indeed, the proportional value of the members of the population of a small jurisdiction will correspond to a value on one of the tails of the overall distribution with finite probability. The result is that, with repeated trails, a small jurisdiction should eventually display a distribution of some characteristic markedly divergent from the distribution of that characteristic in the greater population.

It should be emphasized that this conclusion arises simply from postulating a random flow of persons with salient characteristics across a system of boundaries such that it defines small samples of the overall population moving through an urban area. Given the interaction of these factors, a geographically defined population that is eccentric is some regard must almost inevitably appear at some point in time by the laws of probability. In fact, with repeated trials, the probability of such an occurrence asymptotically approaches one.

At this point in the dynamic sorting process, when eccentricity has emerged, a spatial unit, or jurisdiction, is transformed into a place by the interaction of geography, sociology, demography, and the economy. A transformation occurs such that what had been a random walk of independent trials becomes a series of correlated events, a process operating through time. Random movement is curtailed by information-based sorting at the political boundary (chapter 3). The emergence of place identity interacts with the preferences of settlers, and outcomes of one trial become strong predictors of outcomes of subsequent trials.

This determinism can be expected to extend not only to the immediate place so affected, but to surrounding places as well. It should be clear that when one place population becomes eccentric, the probability that others will become eccentric is increased, if only slightly. By necessity, if a disproportionate number of whites, for instance, are drawn to a particular community, then a disproportionately small number are left to be distributed across the remainder of communities. If only one small jurisdiction is involved, the impact of the rest of the metropolitan area would not be noticeable. But when many jurisdictions attract more than their share of whites (or blacks, or professionals and managers, or college graduates, or traditional families), the proportion of whites in the rest of the area must be reduced.

So one must imagine, in the ideal metropolis of the past, that it is highly improbable that a central city could by random movement alone acquire an eccentric population. The number of persons moving across a central city boundary in any time period is so large that they must be fairly representative of the greater population. However, eccentricities can occur fairly easily in small populations. If a number of small jurisdictions were to become eccentric, and recruitment were engendered at their boundaries, it would produce a complementary distortion in the demography of central cities.

This picture is not entirely inconsistent with what is known of the differences between central cities and suburbs. For instance, to the extent that the outmigration of whites is a response to pull factors in the suburbs (recruitment, one might call it), this probabalistic explanation of population movement is quite compatible with twentieth century developments.

Of course, theory predicts that once a jurisdiction moves out to the tail of the overall distribution of some salient characteristic and the sorting dynamic is engendered, there will be no return to the distribution's mean value. The impetus of the sorting dynamic is to perpetuate eccentricity once it occurs. Persons whose characteristics and preferences match the eccentricities of the community in question will be attracted to it.

This probabalistic argument demonstrates the causal impetus of urban political boundaries. Where eccentricity exists in a jurisdiction, political boundaries serve to perpetuate it. More significantly, compactly drawn boundaries will produce eccentricity even where it has not previously existed—first in smaller jurisdictions, and then, indirectly, in larger ones.

## Asymmetric Population Sorting

Before concluding this chapter, one qualification should be made. It as been argued that preferences are a central element in the process of population sorting supported by political boundaries, but the attempt to satisfy such preferences is constrained by the resource levels of the settlers involved. Settlers comprise a varied group including persons of all socioeconomic strata. Generally, individuals engaged in location search who have abundant resources make choices in response to preferences, while individuals with few resources conform to the decisions that are made by others. "There are certainly conditions such as family finances and market supply which enlarge or restrict the number of choices open to us—from very many to none at all" (Michelson 1977: 14). Eventually, as the level of resources decreases, individuals making locational decisions lose the power to act on their preferences and must simply accept whatever is left after others have made their choices.

This distinction between "choice-makers" and "choice-takers" is important for two reasons. One reason is that the process of population sorting is not neutral with respect to the life chances presented to the households which are sorted. The availability of many types of life chances is mediated by distance and by demography. Those who are isolated in economically moribund areas in the central city and the near suburbs, for instance, may be denied opportunities for jobs, services, and a higher standard of living by the simple fact that economic expansion is occurring in areas physically removed from them (Kasarda 1985, 1983). The segregation and concentration of the poor intensifies social pathologies, aggravating crime, family disintegration, and addiction, and creating an atmosphere of despair (Downs 1981: 52–58). The outmigration of the middle class reinforces the isolation of the underclass, destroying neighborhood norms favoring educational achievement and hard work, and depriving them of role models in the form of individuals who have succeeded by conforming to such norms (Wilson 1987; Lemann 1986a, 1986b). The differential movement of demographic groups and resources causes the system of governments and political boundaries in metropolitan areas to become a stratification system as well (Hill 1974). By understanding the difference between choice-makers and choice-takers, one avoids detaching the sorting done by political boundaries from its social consequences.

The second reason that such a distinction is important is that it creates an asymmetry in the sorting process (see chapter 4). High-resource settlers undertake a different strategy of housing search than low-resource settlers. Their wealth permits them to indulge different preferences than those less advantaged, and they are likely to seek differenct information. The high-resource settler, the choice-maker, is in fact Hirschman's (1970) connoisseur, while the low-resource settler, the choice-taker, is the marginal consumer. The choice-maker surveys the entire metropolitan area seeking enclaves that satisfy his preferences for amenities and life style, thus creating Berry's

(1973) mosaic culture. The choice-taker fills in the spaces that are left. It is the low-resource choice-taker that is susceptible to exclusion at the municipal boundary (Danielson 1976). But exclusion explains only half of the pattern of segregation. It can tell us how low-resource households become clustered in specific areas, but it offers no insight as to how high-resource household become geographically concentrated so that they come to recognize a common interest, incorporate, and begin to wield exclusionary powers. Patterns of differential settlement by race and class represent not only the segregation of the least advantaged, but the aggregation of the most advantaged. The same explanation of population sorting cannot explain both. Thus, in chapter 4, when results indicate that the highly educated and professionals and managers are becoming more segregated by municipality in metropolitan areas, this outcome cannot be explained by referring to exclusion. Preferences and information have to be examined, since such groups have sufficient resources to act from choice rather than bare necessity.

## Conclusion

The argument made in this chapter about population sorting in metropolitan areas, and the role that political fragmentation, and particularly political boundaries, plays in that process, can be summarized in more or less schematic fashion. Individuals and households, in making locational decisions, attempt to satisfy certain preferences. These preferences, bound up with deeply felt concerns about family, security, and life style, cause settlers to seek residential spaces which are relatively homogeneous regarding the racial and socioeconomic characteristics of their populations. This endeavor cannot be supported without information which permits movers to compare preferences with objective conditions in different places. Political boundaries make such information available by defining discrete spatial units which can then be characterized according to the preferences of movers. Indeed, because of the certainty with which these units are defined, and the interaction that such precise boundaries encourage between geography, political power and publicly provided services, economic activity, and the social characteristics of residents, political boundaries are quite instrumental in creating place identity. Settlers are able to react to strongly characterized places, and the interaction between place and settler preferences has produced the mosaic culture.

# 3

## An Information-Based Model of Jurisdictional Tipping

Chapters 1 and 2 present a theory of the importance of political boundaries to the process of metropolitan segregation by race and class. Chapter 2 argues that political boundaries are not simply implicated in this process, but that on occasion they provide the causal impetus.

This chapter presents a formalization of the theory. A dynamic, difference equation model is used to represent the process of jurisdictional transition. The model is non-linear, and is driven by an interdependence between peculiarities or eccentricities occurring in jurisdictional populations and the amount of information supplied to persons making locational decisions. Political boundaries permit the unambiguous identification of spatial units; and they also make it possible for discrete spatial units to be associated with populations of determinate socioeconomic and demographic characteristics. This chapter further argues that the substantive importance of the tipping point is that it represents a change in the perceptions of the relevant spatial unit on the part of persons making locational decisions. What they had once held to be a "white, middle class area," for instance comes to be considered something else. The tipping point is the point at which a change takes place in the way people *think* about an objectively defined area, the point at which their sense of the place changes.

### Racial Transition and Tipping-Point Models

A great deal of literature indicates that once black penetration of geographic units occurs, complete transition and succession is nearly inevitable (Massey and Mullan, 1984; Berry et al. 1976; Orfield, 1978; Duncan and Duncan, 1957). The repeatedly demonstrated instability of integrated neighborhoods has prompted a number of analysts to offer the "neighborhood-tipping" explanation of neighborhood racial change (Steinnes 1977; Grodzins 1957; Schelling 1978). According to this theory, once the proportion black of the population of a spatial unit reaches a certain point, an irreversible process of neighborhood transition is engendered.

Both Steinnes and Molotch (1972) suggest that residential mobility of whites and distance of a previously white neighborhood from residential concentrations of blacks are important factors in understanding neighborhood racial transition. Mobility, obviously, creates the vacancies into which blacks can move. Many places do not undergo racial transition, however, even though mobility in these places may be high. Molotch (1972) offers the example of a Chicago neighborhood with mobility rates similar to those in South Shore: South Shore could not fend off racial transition in spite of substantial efforts by neighborhood groups and public and private insitutitions, while transition was not a serious possibility in its counterpart neighborhood.

Steinnes (1977) and Molotch (1972) cite the interaction of residential mobility with distance from predominantly black neighborhoods. Racial transition is more likely to occur in places near to existing black residential areas in which significant numbers of vacancies are created by white mobility. It is legitimate to ask, however, why distance should be such an important consideration in understanding *black* residential mobility. Other minority groups are not so spatially restricted in their search for housing (Massey and Mullan 1984).

In addition to mobility and distance, Molotch invokes the dual housing market (Molotch 1972; Duncan and Duncan 1957: 7; Downs 1981: 86–102). Blacks have fewer housing options than do whites because of discrimination. They can procure housing only in the limited number of markets that are open to them, typically markets that are in ghetto areas or nearby. Because of the relative scarcity of housing alternatives, blacks will pay a premium for housing.

This picture of racial transition, then, is a composite of residential mobility, distance from black neighborhoods, and the dual housing market. Discrimination against blacks leads them to seek housing predominantly in areas which they perceive to offer some promise of success—areas which are traditionally near ghettoes. They are willing to outbid whites for such housing. All that is required to insure neighborhood transition is a white mobility rate greater than zero.

A critical factor in understanding racial transition in spatial units is the process by which such units shift from the white market to the black market. Several observers indicate that this shift is principally a matter of changing perceptions among the actors involved. Berry and associates comment: "Because Park Forest has been well publicized as an integrated community and many of the suburbs around it are known to be highly resistant to black immigration, increasing numbers of blacks began to seek homes within its confines" (1976: 241). Similarly, Molotch indicates that one of the prerequisites for racial change is the perception by blacks that it is possible to obtain housing in an integrated or a white area (Molotch 1972: 17).

It is not too great a distortion of this literature to say that it posits a model of neighborhood transition predicated upon a crucial point at which relevant actors perceive that a spatial unit has become part of the black housing market. The tipping point represents the level at which the perceptions of persons making locational decisions change. The quintessential significance of the tipping point is that it represents a fundamental change in cognition respecting the spatial unit in question.

## Locational Preferences and Racial Antipathies

Individual thinking about places is likely to occur and be most fully articulated when households are engaged in housing search and the making of locational decisions—that is, when they are "moving" (W. Frey 1979). It is precisely when the household is making a locational decision that the definition and description of geographic units ("places") becomes salient. It is also at this point that another cognitive element, *preferences* about the characteristics of places considered as residences, comes into play. The moving process at the household level is an explicit area of focus in this chapter because: (1) it provides the nexus in which perceptions of places and preferences about places are mutually crystallized; and because (2) the great patterns of segregation and aggregation that are apparent in metropolitan areas result from decisions made at the household level in the process of moving.

In choosing a particular location, the members of a household are trying to satisfy manifold preferences. These preferences commonly are thought to concern the quality of housing, the provision of services and the imposition of fees and taxes, the amenities, security, and quality of life available in the neighborhood, the status equated with the location, and the race, social class, and ethnicity of neighbors. Of course, to know the motives behind any particular location decision would require one to question the specific household involved in that move. But analyses of survey data, as well as the literature cited above, suggest the nature of a constellation of preferences that is pervasive among the residents of metropolitan areas, and that has very significant implications for residential patterns.

Surveys taken over a period of decades support the conclusion that racial antipathy persists between blacks and whites. This statement may be controversial in light of answers to some survey questions that indicate a dramatic increase in white tolerance for blacks (Schuman, Steeh, and Bobo 1985). Whites now show overwhelming approval of principles of racial equality in employment, equality in civil rights, integration of schools, and so on. In spite of this postwar trend toward support for principles of racial equality, whites are much less likely to approve of integration when they are presented with the concrete alternative of having blacks as neighbors; are less approving of equality when it is presented in terms of concrete action; and are still likely, in large numbers, to agree that blacks have a number of objectionable personal traits. (The literature supporting these contentions is discussed in detail in chapter 4.)

To this point, I have presented evidence in the social science literature that the "tipping point" in the process of neighborhood transition represents the point at which a change occurs in perceptions about that neighborhood. I also argue that substantial numbers of whites continue to prefer that their residences not be near residential concentrations of blacks. These factors do not adequately explain the process of racial transition. They merely suggest a further question. Given the importance of the way in which various actors think about spatial units, what is it that structures their thinking?

## Boundedness and Residential Tipping

American metropolitan areas are highly fragmented and jurisdictional fragmentation is paralleled by the spatial differentiation of racial, ethnic, and socioeconomic groups. This differentiation can be partially explained by invoking exclusionary powers; but exclusion alone cannot account for the persistence of white, middle class communities in the face of the high residential mobility and rapid population turnover that characterizes modern urban areas. A community that was entirely successful in excluding blacks would disappear in fairly short order if it were unable to attract whites to replace residents that died or moved away. A complete understanding of sociospatial differentiation requires a theory of recruitment as a complement to exclusion. Treatments of recruitment tend to talk about motives—preferences for services or social and racial antipathies—that propel the recruitment dynamic without specifically discussing how individuals identify places that are compatible with their preferences. That is to say, they assume that individuals have the information that is prerequisite to acting upon their preferences (Tiebout 1956; Schelling 1978). This approach to the information component of the recruitment dynamic is unsatisfactory in light of the fact that the type of information available to settlers and the way it is provided may well condition patterns of the distribution of persons and resources and, through them, a number of urban outcomes.

The frequency with which urban political boundaries are cited in the literature of urban fragmentation as elements structuring urban spatial segregation has been noted in chapter 1 (Skogan 1977; Stein 1987; Molotch 1972). Boundaries are an essential, though implicit, element in Tiebout's (1956) treatment of residential mobility. Boundedness and bounding were integral components in the human ecology approach developed by Burgess, Park, and Mackenzie (Park 1952b: 201).

Boundedness is an essential element of tipping-point analyses, as witness Schelling's (1978) bounded neighborhood model; though it is rarely explicitly discussed in their articulation. Without the prior existence of discrete spatial units to be "tipped", the meaning of the tipping-point is unclear. As an essential prerequisite to the development of his understanding of racial transition based on individual preferences, Schelling stipulates that there be "a common definition of the neighborhood and its boundaries—a person is either inside or outside" (1978: 155).

How, specifically, one may ask, is a person to know if he is either inside or outside the spatial unit in question?

The answer to this question is problematic when the spatial unit is an urban neighborhood. It has been noted previously (chapter 2) that in most cases, no agency establishes authoritatively, beyond dispute, the location of boundaries between neighborhoods. Neighborhoods, in fact, are not formally constituted—they have no formal, unambiguous boundaries. Quoting the National Commission on Neighborhoods, Downs (1981: 13) notes that "in the last analysis, each neighborhood is what the inhabitants think it is." Most evidence indicates, however, that the inhabitants of neighborhoods are seldom in agreement about the location of boundaries, or even about their neighborhood's name (Hunter 1975; Form et al. 1954). "No one definition [of neighborhood] has come into widespread acceptance among neighborhood residents themselves, neighborhood organizations, or academic analysts" (Downs 1981: 13). In fact, the preponderance of the human ecology literature argues that "a common definition of neighborhood" is generally unobtainable.

Social scientists, explicitly or implicitly, point to boundaries as elements structuring the process in which persons and resources are distributed across spatial units. Boundaries are an integral part of the cognitive map of metropolitan areas that people use to make locational decisions. Many boundaries are ambiguous, however. The superiority of political boundaries is that they are objectively defined and hence provide a more certain reference than informal boundaries. The exact location of the southern boundary of South Shore may be uncertain, but there is no uncertainty about the boundaries of Skokie or Calumet or Markham or Wheaton. Settlers in urban areas must make reference to boundaries in order to exercise their locational preferences, and political boundaries are the best boundaries of all because they unambiguously define discrete spatial units.

## Model Assumptions

All of these elements—perceptions, preferences, and boundaries—come together in the locational calculus of individual settlers. The preceding review of literature suggests that certain assumptions about the process of locational search and choice as it is carried on by households can be reasonably made. These assumptions are:

1. Persons making locational decisions have preferences about the characteristics of the location that they will ultimately choose. These preferences concern quality of housing, security and freedom from crime, attitudes of neighbors toward upkeep of their property, behavior of residents in public areas such as parks and streets, and quality of services and facilities. Preferences of this sort frequently crystalize around considerations of race and socioeconomic class. The survey evidence of persistent racial antipathy has been previously noted, and the persistence of residential segregation (a likely manifestation of such antipathy) should also be noted (Massey and Denton 1987). Anderson (1985) notes the tendency of whites to equate the presence of blacks with high crime rates; and whites are also apt to associate blacks with drug trafficking and abuse, sexual laxity, distasteful public behavior, poverty, poor schools, and so on (Danielson 1976: 11–12).

2. A jurisdictional population that is in all salient respects like the greater population in a metropolitan area provides a settler with no cues for making a locational decision. If she is interested in finding an area that is compatible with her racial, ethnic, religious, or class identity, she will have no strong preference regarding a nondistinctive jurisdictional population. This is simply in the nature of preferences. If preferences tend to crystallize around considerations of race and class, then spatial units will be accepted or rejected on the basis of their distinctiveness with respect to these characteristics. Less distinctive areas will be of little interest to persons making decisions on this basis, and population sorting in these areas will be residual to any dynamic based on individual preferences respecting race and class.

3. Persons making locational decisions need information about places within a housing market in order to act on their preferences. Making such a decision involves

—defining or identifying discrete geographic units

—attributing to these units socioeconomic identities

—selecting geographic units worthy of more detailed examination

—choosing a location in one of these units

In other words, acting upon preferences about places requires the formation of perceptions about these places, and the formation of perceptions depends upon the receipt of information. Acquiring information has costs, and settlers face fairly severe constraints of time and resources on their ability to meet such costs. Given such constraints, settlers will be most likely to accept information that is unambiguous and of relatively low cost.

4. The jurisdictional fragmentation of American metropolitan areas, because it eventuates in the *bounding* of geographic units, provides an easily adaptable cognitive framework which permits persons engaged in residential search to generate low cost, unambiguous information. The initial task in gathering information about housing options is to reduce the undifferentiated urban geography to a more manageable set of discrete geographic subunits (Smith and Clark 1980). The political fragmentation of American metropolitan areas aids settlers faced with this task by providing a ready-made system of boundaries and discrete spatial units. It permits settlers to define, at little cost, "discrete subareas, each of which is relatively homogeneous with respect to the chance of finding an acceptable vacancy" (Smith and Clark 1980).

Collectively, these assumptions incorporate concern for what have been previously identified as important factors in the process of racial transition—the division of urban geography into discrete units, the perceptions of those units by individuals, and the preferences that these individuals bring to the process of housing search. These factors considered together suggest that housing search should be understood as an information intensive process, and that the system of political boundaries that subdivide the metropolis should be seen as an information system. If these assumptions are reasonable, then they suggest a formal model of racial transition of the sort articulated in the remainder of this chapter.

## A Model of Demographic Transition in Jurisdictions

Here the concept of population eccentricity is introduced. The eccentricity of any jurisdictional population is the degree to which that population differs from the metropolitan population overall. Eccentricity is measured by measuring $C_t$, a deviation from the SMSA mean proportion of some salient characteristic—race, for example—in a jurisdictional population at time **t**. It is essential to be clear about what $C_t$ represents. If $S$ represents the proportion of the SMSA population that is black, and $S_j$ represents the proportion black in a jurisdictional population, then $C_t$ for any jurisdiction is equal to the difference of $S$ and $S_j$ during the time period $t$. Note that $C_t$ is expressed in the same proportional metric as are $S_j$ and $S$.

(1) $C_t = S - S_{jt}$

The value of $C$ at a time period $(t + 1)$ is a function of $C$ in the previous time period. Specifically the value of $C$ at a given time period is a function of its value in the previous time period plus an increase of some proportion of $C$ resulting from the information provided by political boundaries. This information permits discrete spatial units to be identified, and also permits the populations of those units to be characterized in demographic and socioeconomic terms. Hence

(2) $\Delta C_t = iC_t$

or, by disaggregation of the change operator delta

(3) $C_{t+1} = iC_t + C_t$

Again, the parameter $i$ represents the information that is supplied by political boundaries to persons making locational decisions. The bounds of $i$ are zero and one, since it is assumed that information alone will not cause $C_t$ to double or disappear in one time period.

(4) $0 \le i \le 1$

It also seems reasonable to assume that in any time period a certain number of blacks move out of the jurisdiction for reasons that are not discretionary. Life-cycle changes, changes in job status, and so on, can generate such nondiscretionary moves. For the most part, persons moving out of necessity are not expressing preferences about the racial makeup of a population. Therefore, the amount of information about racial composition conveyed by a political boundary is irrelevant to them. These defections are represented by the parameter $f$.

(5) $C_{t+1} = iC_t - fC_t + C_t$

The parameter $f$ is also expressed as a proportion of $C_t$ and is bounded by zero and one by the same logic that pertains to $i$.

(6) $0 \le f \le 1$

Finally, it is safe to assume that $C_t$ is influenced by exogenous shocks to the system. An urban renewal project may eliminate areas of low income housing, or an annexation may radically alter the socioeconomic or demographic composition of the population. Such events are represented by the parameter $K$.

(7) $C_{t+1} = iC_t - fC_t + C_t + K_t$

The K parameter is expressed in the proportional metric of $C_t$.

In words, equation (7) states that the deviation from the metropolitan norm in the proportion black of a jurisdictional population depends on the magnitude of the deviation in the preceding time period; the capacity of the jurisdictional boundaries to convey information about racial composition to persons for whom it is salient; and the rate of turnover among blacks that is not affected by information. This entire dynamic is subject to exogenous shocks.

By Assumption 2, boundaries convey no information about the populations they define if these populations are not in any way distinctive. That is to say, the magnitude of the parameter $i$ depends upon the degree to which, in this case, the proportion black in the smaller population departs from the mean proportion in the SMSA. As the population becomes more identifiable in terms of the presence or absence of blacks, the boundary of the jurisdiction conveys more information to those for whom jurisdictional racial distinctiveness is pertinent. Thus

(8) $i = g(C_t)$

$i$ is a function of $C_t$.

These theoretical considerations impose certain requirements upon the functional form of the relationship between $i$ and $C_t$. Specifically, the value of $i$ must be one, indicating that boundaries convey as much information as they can, when $C_t$ goes to its upper or lower limit. These requirements and the nature of the relationship between $C_t$ and $i$ are graphically portrayed in Figure 3.1

For the purposes of this figure, a value of 0.3 was assigned to $S$ the mean proportion black in the metropolitan population. Therefore, when $S_{jt}$, the proportion black of the jurisdictional population, is also equal to 0.3, $C_t$ is equal to zero. Since the system state $C_t$ is expressed as a proportion, the range within which it can vary in this instance is $[-0.3, (1 - 0.3)]$. In other words, the upper limit of $C_t$ is 0.7, and its lower limit is $-0.3$. The figure demonstrates that $i$ equals zero when $C_t$ equals zero, and has a

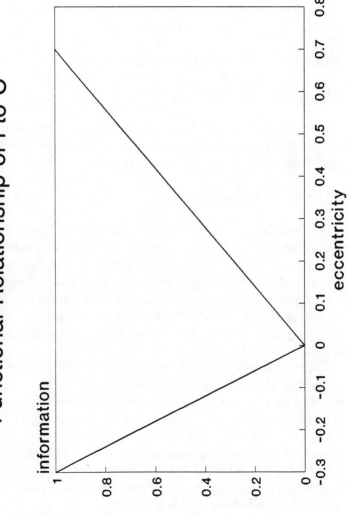

Figure 3.1
Functional Relationship of i to C

value of one when $C_t$ goes to either of its limits. A functional form for $i = g(C_t)$ is available which meets these requirements. (Technical details are included in the Appendix).

The model, then, has the following form:

(9) $C_{t+1} = i_t C_t - fC_t + C_t + K_t$

which by algebraic manipulation becomes

(10) $C_{t+1} = (i_t - f + 1)C_t + K_t$

It should be noted that when one substitutes for $i_t$ using the function described above, the result is a quadratic equation in $C_t$ of the following form:

(11) $\Delta C_t = aC^2_t + bC_t + K_t$

Does this system have any equilibria? This can be determined by using the quadratic formula and setting $\Delta C_t$ equal to zero (See Huckfeldt, Kohfeld, and Likens 1982: 39–40). By substituting specific values for parameters (see Appendix) and employing this technique, one finds that the system is at equilibrium at the following values of $C_t$ (remembering that these values express *deviation* from the SMSA mean): 0, $-0.027$, 0.064.

There are a number of methods for analyzing the behavior of the system over time to see if it converges to equilibrium or goes to a limit. The one used here is straightforward and depends on an examination of the term $(i_t - f + 1)C_t$ which occurs on the right side of the equation. (For present purposes, $K$ is disregarded. More will be said of it later.) It becomes clear that the growth of $C_t$ depends upon the values assigned to the parameters $i_t$ and $f$. The following are apparent:

(12) when $i_t > f$, $(i_t - f + 1) > 1$

(13) when $i_t < f$, $(i_t - f + 1) < 1$

Thus when $i_t > f$, repeated multiplication of the system state $C_t$ by $(i_t - f + 1)$ causes the magnitude of $C_t$ to increase in successive time periods, and it goes to its limit. The opposite is true when $i_t < f$. Under this condition, $C_t$ converges to equilibrium.

The crucial importance of the values of $i_t$ and $f$ can be graphically illustrated by modifying Figure 3.1. In Figure 3.2, a distance is laid off on the $i$ axis corresponding to the value of the $f$ parameter. This distance is represented by the line $f$. For the purposes of this demonstration, $f$ has been assigned a value of 0.09. Additional vertical lines have been added at the values of $-0.027$ and $0.064$ on the $C_t$ axis. These are the equilibrium values produced by the previous examination of the quadratic equation in $C_t$. (They are consistent with the assumption about the value of the $f$ parameter since they were computed using an $f$ value of 0.09.)

Significantly, the figure indicates that the line $f$ crosses the $(C_t)$ line at the two non-zero equilibria produced by previous computations. In other words, as an examination of the $(i_t - f + 1)\, C_t$ term indicates, the system is at equilibrium when the values of $i$ and $f$ are equal. As this term further indicates, however, these equilibria are unstable. For all values of $C_t$ described by the inequality $-0.027 < C_t < 0.064$, the value of $i_t$ is less than $f$. Therefore, for these values of $C_t$ the system is convergent to the stable equilibrium at $C_t = 0$. The square surrounding the origin represents the region within which the system is convergent. On the other hand, any value of $C_t$ lying outside this range will cause the system to go to its upper and lower limit because for these values, $i_t$ is greater than $f$. When the system reaches its upper limit, all members of the jurisdictional population are black. At the lower limit, blacks are completely absent in the jurisdictional population.

A further demonstration of the equilibrium properties of the model is given by Figure 3.3. Initial values of $C_t$ were set to $-0.025$ and to $-0.03$. Since the lower border of the region of stability for the model lies at approximately

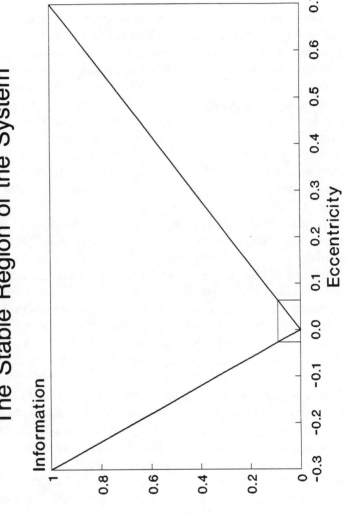

Figure 3.2
The Stable Region of the System

−0.027, the time path for the former starting condition should converge toward zero; and the time path of the later should tend toward the lower limit. Computer iteration of the model for these two initial values indicates the time paths shown in Figure 3.3. In fact, these time paths conform to expectations.

This model is relatively faithful to its assumptions and the theory from which they are derived. The motivating assumptions of the model are that persons engaged in location search have preferences, and that the attempt to satisfy those preferences requires information. Political boundaries supply the minimal prerequisite for gathering information about places—the ability to distinguish one place from another. The heart of the model is the interaction of discrete geography with culture, sociology, economy, and polity. This interaction has been presented previously as the essence of "place". As this interaction proceeds, politically defined spatial units acquire place identity, and it produces an entrenched sorting dynamic.

## Salience and Jurisdictional Population Dynamics

For convenience sake, the recursive form of the model is reproduced here.

$$(13)\ \ C_{t+1} = (i_t - f + 1)\, C_t + K_t$$

What is known of the model's behavior can be summarized briefly. Since $i$ has been defined as a function of $C_t$, the model is non-linear. Algebraic manipulation yields a quadratic equation in $C_t$. Cursory analysis of the model indicates that it is locally stable in the region where the value of the parameter $f$ exceeds the value of $i$. The substantive interpretation is that the ebb and flow of persons across a particular jurisdiction must result in eccentricity that is greater than what might be expected from random migration patterns alone. When that degree of eccentricity is reached, the amount of information conveyed by the boundary dominates the effect of normal gains and losses.

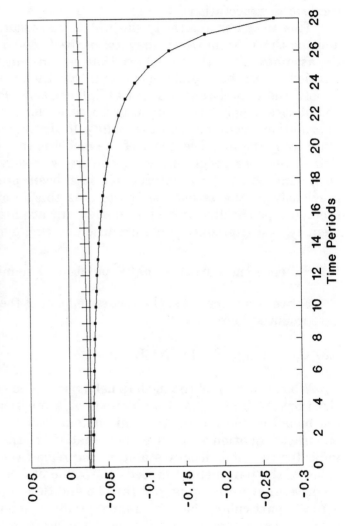

Figure 3.3
Two Initial Values of C

The system goes to its upper or lower limit, depending on the polarity of the initial shock. That is to say, a jurisdictional population is produced in which all members bear the relevant characteristic, or in which it is totally absent.

The behavior of the system in this respect is dependent upon the salience of the characteristic—race, ethnicity, socioeconomic status, religious affiliation—in question. When such a characteristic is highly salient, the random movement of persons across jurisdictional boundaries need only produce a slight eccentricity for the information-based sorting dynamic to be activated. On the other hand, when a characteristic has relatively little salience, random movements can result in a substantial presence of the characteristic in a jurisdictional population without activating the sorting dynamic and, in turn, triggering jurisdictional transition.

For instance, Massey and Mullan (1984) report that small concentrations of blacks in residential areas are sufficient to engender transition and succession. Hispanics may be present in an area in substantial numbers, however, without any inevitable transition being engendered. In such a situation, the presence of Hispanics is not as salient to whites as the presence of blacks. Movement across boundaries remains random in the presence of large proportions of Hispanics, while random movement is quickly curtailed by the presence of rather small proportions of blacks. The result is that an area with a large number of Hispanics can continue to attract anglos, while an area with a rather small number of blacks ceases to attract whites altogether.

Differences in salience of this sort can be represented in the model by manipulating the value of the $f$ parameter. When the value of $f$ is large, the proportion of a jurisdictional population bearing the relevant characteristic must depart substantially from the SMSA mean before boundaries begin to convey information regarding that characteristic (that is, $C_t$ must be large). In terms of the behavior of the system, this means simply that the area within which it is stable is greatly increased. Much larger fluctuations in the proportions bearing the characteristic are required to jar the system out of equilibrium and send it toward one of its limits.

For instance, if it is estimated from an examination of census tracts in various stages of transition that movement in and out of tracts remains random up to the point that forty percent of the tract population is Hispanic, one would assign a value to the $f$ parameter in the model of 0.4. The results of changing the value of $f$ in this fashion, while leaving all other values the same as in the previous demonstration, are displayed in Figure 3.4. This increase in the value of $f$ shifts the two unstable equilibria outward to $-0.12$ and $0.28$. A cursory examination of Figure 3.4 reveals that the stable region of the system has been greatly increased. This increase in stability conforms nicely to the perception that areas can tolerate relatively wide fluctuations in the size of the Hispanic population without being "tipped."

Understanding $f$ to represent the ceiling value for random movement is, in fact, a fairly faithful application of the concept of salience. When it is said that characteristics are salient to settlers, this means exactly that they pay attention to them. Small variations are closely scrutinized and figure significantly in decision-making. Factors that are not salient are "disconnected" from decisions. They can fluctuate randomly without limit and no action logically follows on the part of decision-makers.

### Implications of the Dynamic Model for Segregation and Racial Policy

This model indicates that jurisdictional populations are likely to be unstable in any intermediate proportional range for any characteristic such as race which is highly salient for persons making locational decisions. This instability results from the narrowness of the stable region of the system under the condition of high salience. Relatively small random shocks to the system are apt to jar it out of its stable region toward one of its limits.

Substantively, the import of the model is that integrated jurisdictional populations *should* be unstable. So long as household preferences about residences are predicated on race; and so long as political boundaries permit households to identify discrete spatial units and characterize them with respect to household preferences, the tipping of racially mixed municipalities in urban areas will not be an unexpected, but a predictable, phenomenon.

The model also indicates that polar jurisdictional populations—those that are practically all white or all black—should be highly stable. They can absorb substantial shocks and still return to their polar status. White municipalities will tend to remain white, and black municipalities to remain black.

This property of the model is relevant to what might be called the "economic" argument about segregation. It is sometimes argued that segregation results as a function of individual preferences and economic demand. People live in the places they prefer to the extent that they have the resources to get residences in these places. If this results in segregation, the causes are to be found not in discriminatory policies, but in differences in individual resources and preferences. If it is suggested that discriminatory policies have been common in the United States, the reply is that these policies were substantially eliminated by litigation and legislation in the nineteen-fifties and -sixties. By this argument, remedial policies are not justified because discriminatory policies are no longer in place, and because remedial policies interfere with the autonomy of citizens to live in communities of their choosing.

The dynamic model, however, suggests that discriminatory actions need not be frequent to result in metropolitan areas that are highly segregated by jurisdiction. Policy decisions in the past which have resulted in the creation of racially polar municipalities will be perpetuated by the tendency of the boundaries to structure the information that is available to persons making locational decisions. Consequently, it can be plausibly argued that policies that imposed discriminatory patterns in the past are still exerting their affect unless explicit action has been taken to correct them.

The conceptualization of the residual term $K$ is relevant to this point. $K$ represents random exogenous shocks to the system. In previous evaluation of the model, it has been assigned a value of zero because, being defined as a random shock, there seemed no justification for assigning it one value rather than another. The value of $K$ in any time period is idiosyncratically determined, and it was omitted from prior consideration for simplicity's sake.

The term $K$ refers to a class of events that cannot be accounted for within the theoretical framework of this chapter. These are events that radically alter the composition of jurisdictional populations with regard to some salient characteristic. Boundary changes, for instance, may dramatically change the proportion of a jurisdiction that is black, or wealthy, or well-educated. The system proceeds through successive time periods according to its own internal logic until such an event shocks it into an entirely different configuration. Since nothing in the system logic accounts for it, it would seem more justifiable to consider an occurrence of this type as a hiatus in the path of the system (See Sprague 1981 for a similar use of the residual term in a dynamic system.) In the succeeding period, the value of $C$ should be thought of as a new initial condition ($C_0$).

The substantive import of this conceptualization of $K$ should be clear when one recalls that with nonlinear first order difference equations, the initial condition of the system determines the point at which the system comes to rest (Huckfeldt, Kohfeld, and Likens 1982). If $C_0$ falls within the stable neighborhood of a local equilibrium, it converges to that point. Otherwise it goes to infinity or to its limit.

Substantively, exogenous shocks of the sort represented by $K$ can dramatically alter the racial or class composition of a jurisdiction. There are a number of examples

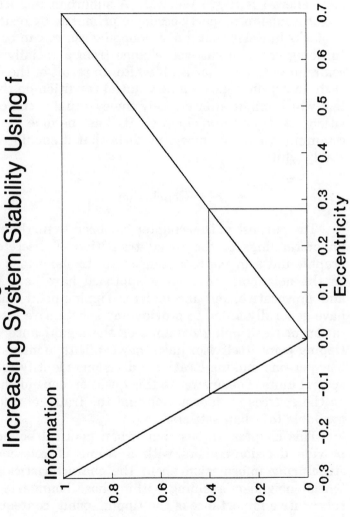

Figure 3.4
Increasing System Stability Using f

of such shocks in the history of United States. For instance, programs of economic redevelopment have had a well documented tendency to proceed by first demolishing-black residential areas, giving rise to the dictum that "urban renewal is negro removal." A suburban municipality might condemn property occupied primarily by residences of blacks in order that a new shopping center can be built. In doing so, it might well change from a racially mixed community to one that is all white. In terms of the model, such an action imposes a new initial condition on the system which might alter entirely the eventual racial composition of that municipality. It has become a polar community, and the model predicts that it should remain stably white.

## Conclusion

The purpose of this chapter has been to further refine understandings of the racial transition of discrete geographic units in metropolitan areas. Explanations based on the neighborhood tipping approach have been useful and provocative, but incomplete. Tipping-point analyses have generally failed to provide any substantive interpretation of the tipping dynamic or the significance of the tipping point itself. Nor have they explicitly demonstrated how persons making locational decisions identify relevant spatial units. The answer to this question depends heavily on the sources of information and the frame of reference available to urban settlers.

This chapter argues that urban political boundaries provide decision-makers with a frame of reference for structuring information about the characteristics of potential neighbors residing within those boundaries. The substantive importance of the tipping-point, consequently, is that it represents the point at which the perceptions of settlers regarding an area change. The importance of political boundaries in this process is that they provide the objective definition of geographic areas that is prerequisite to thinking and decision-making in these terms.

## Appendix

Following is the specific functional form of the interaction of the parameter $i_t$ and the system state $C_t$;

(1) $i_t = x|C_t| + y(1 - k - C_t) + z$

The value of the coefficients in equation (1) is specified by the following equations:

(2) $x = \dfrac{1}{2k(1-k)}$

(3) $y = \dfrac{-(2k-1)}{2k(1-k)}$

(4) $z = \dfrac{2k-1}{2k}$

The constant $k$ in these equations corresponds to the population mean value $S$ in the text, and is assigned a value of 0.3. In the first demonstration in the text (Figure 3.2), parameters and coefficients are assigned the following values:

$f = 0.09$
$x = 2.381$
$y = 0.952$
$z = -0.667$

In the second demonstration (Figure 3.4), the value assigned to $f$ is 0.40.

# 4

# Public Policy and Patterns of Residential Segregation*

This book is concerned with the structure of relationships between the preferences of persons searching for locations, the objective characteristics of spatial units, and the nature of the information that is available to settlers about spatial units. It argues that these relationships are mediated by the existence of political boundaries which can be readily adapted to serve as cognitive maps, and which are then used to provide the nexus between preferences and objective conditions. Boundaries permit those engaged in location search to characterize spatial units with regard to their preferences, and thus to make decisions among spatial units.

The tendency of boundaries to perform this function has been increased by public policy produced from the late 1940s to the seventies and early eighties. In the presence of a persistent aversion to blacks on the part of whites, public policy has not ameliorated residential segregation. Rather, it has restructured it by presenting these whites with altered incentives and institutional forms. The result

* This chapter originally appeared in the *Western Political Quarterly*, volume 42, number 4, pages 651–677. Reprinted by permission of the University of Utah, copyright holder.

has been a change in the geographic pattern of, rather than a reduction in, residential segregation.

Black geographic segregation is, at least in part, a manifestation of a continuing aversion to blacks on the part of whites (Bobo, Schuman, and Steeh 1986). The measurement of segregation is problematic owing to the many facets of the concept (Stearns and Logan 1986; Massey and Denton 1988b). Nevertheless, most studies conclude that segregation, however it may be measured, has not decreased notably in metropolitan areas (for instance, Massey and Denton 1987).

The persistence of residential segregation stands as an indictment of nearly forty years of civil rights policy. The federal courts and the Congress of the United States have been engaged in an ongoing formulation of policy designed to limit racial discrimination. Governmental attempts to open opportunities to blacks have produced notable successes in employment and voting. In spite of repeated initiatives in the area of housing, however, few places in the metropolis can be said to be stably integrated (Massey and Mullan 1984; Berry et al. 1976).

An important element of the general argument of this chapter is the contention that many whites prefer not to live near residential concentrations of blacks. There is, therefore, a continuing interest on the part of whites to find residences that do not expose them to blacks.

This chapter presents the argument that public policy has been able to redirect this interest, but not to thwart it. Civil rights policy has substantially dismantled neighborhood level, or "intrajurisdictional", mechanisms of segregation. But federal court policy has reinforced devices which support interjurisdictional racial segregation. If neighborhood level segregative mechanisms are removed while municipal level segregative mechanisms are left intact, municipal borders should gradually become racial and class borders as well. A change in patterns of segregation of this sort would entail no necessary change in the overall level of segregation.

This chapter first reviews evidence of continuing antipathy of whites towards blacks. Then research which attempts to measure metropolitan segregation is reviewed. Subsequently, the developments which have led to the weakening of neighborhood level segregative devices are recounted, and then developments which support segregation on various grounds among juridictions are discussed. The central hypothesis of this chapter is that the summary impact of these two lines of public policy, in the presence of continuing white aversion to blacks, should be a shift in geographic patterns of segregation. Analysis of variance results for municipalities in Cook County, Illinois, and Los Angeles County, California, are then presented which demonstrate that, in these two metropolitan counties, segregation by race and socioeconomic status has become a jurisdictional, rather than a neighborhood level, phenomenon. Finally, processes by which changes in policy and changes in patterns of segregation in metropolitan areas may be linked are discussed.

## Whites' Continuing Aversion to Blacks

A principal argument made in this chapter is that whites continue to be averse to contact with blacks, particularly in their neighborhoods. Survey data indicate that the numbers of whites who are overtly willing to express hostility or distaste for blacks, or to deny them equal chances in various social and political situations have decreased. Nevertheless, a large number of whites continue to make such overt expressions (Sniderman and Tetlock 1986a). According to a Harris national survey taken in 1978, one half to one quarter of Americans agree that 'blacks tend to have less ambition than whites'; that blacks 'breed crime'; that blacks 'have less native intelligence than whites'; that blacks 'want to live off the handout'; that 'blacks are more violent than whites'. Most pertinent for present concerns, twenty-five percent of Americans agree that "white people have a right to keep blacks out of their neighborhoods, and blacks should respect that right.") When asked if homeowners should be able to choose not to sell to blacks, forty-seven percent answered that they should (Sniderman and Tetlock 1986a: 143). These figures quite possibly underestimate the presence of racial antipathy since whites may have learned that racially critical remarks are "socially unacceptable" (Jackman 1978, 1981; Jackman and Muha 1984).

Bobo, Schuman, and Steeh (1986) report that public acceptance for the *principle* of open housing has increased to over 90%; but public support for specific government programs *implementing* open housing is much lower (46% peak value). Although most whites would approve of one black household of similar education and income moving into the neighborhood, public approval for blacks moving in in substantial numbers is much lower (90% and 48% respectively).

Schuman and Bobo (1988) find white opposition to potential black neighbors to be complex, including, among other things, significant opposition to federal government coercion to accomplish racially open neighborhoods. A clear component of such opposition, however, is racial aversion—"a second general conclusion is that there is also an important element of personal prejudice against blacks in white opposition to open-housing laws" (Schuman and Bobo 1988: 295).

Farley et al. (1978), presented survey respondents with graphic representations which portrayed a hypothetical neighborhood of fifteen house-shapes. Mixed neighborhoods were represented by graphics in which an appropriate number of house shapes had been blackened. Using this method of presentation rather than questions about abstract values, the authors found considerable white resistance to residential integration. Twenty-five percent of whites would not feel comfortable if one neighborhood household in fifteen were black. In a half-black neighborhood, 72% of whites would be uncomfortable. Forty percent of whites would move from an area that was half black, and 64% would move from a majority black area. One half of whites said they would not move into an area that was 20% black.

Persistent white aversion to blacks is likely to be most manifest in the selection of residences. Myrdal (1944) observed that whites are most averse to those contacts with blacks which challenge white status and social distancing (see also Berry et al. 1976). Massey and Mullan (1984) note the critical importance of residence as a dimension of racial separation. White aversion to contact with blacks with respect to residential choices is evident in the fact that, considerations of housing quality and amenities being equal, demand for housing is depressed when that housing is located near concentrations of blacks (Palmquist 1984).

## Persistent Segregation

Studies conducted in the nineteen-sixties, nineteen-seventies, and nineteen-eighties have not found a general reduction in residential segregation. The most encouraging reports have been those that cite small reductions in index-of-dissimilarity (D) values for varying samples of American metropolitan areas (Van Valey, Roof, and Wilcox 1977; Sorenson, Taeuber, and Hollingsworth 1974; Taeuber and Taeuber 1965). Massey and Denton (1987) reported declines in racial segregation in the SMSAs of the West. In the Midwest and Northeast, however, where the majority of blacks live, there has been no lessening of segregation.

Other studies reported either no change or increases in the values of various indices of segregation, and no change in patterns of residential segregation in the wake of policies promoting integration (J. Farley 1983; Winsberg 1983). Black suburbanization, though it is found to have increased, is also found to have replicated patterns of ghettoization existing in central cities (R. Farley 1970; Logan and Schneider 1984; Stahura 1988). Massey and Denton (1987) found that there are still substantial barriers to black suburbanization. Berry et al. (1976) reviewed findings that black-occupied housing rarely reverts to white ownership, and that there are very few areas which are integrated in the sense that they attract both black and white prospective residents. Importantly, at least one study (Stein 1987) reported that segregation by race, education, income, and age increases with the number of municipal governments in SMSAs (though only the coefficient for education is significant at the .05 level).

### Contemporary Developments in Judicial Policy: Promoting Integration

In the period immediately following World War II and continuing through the 1960s, U.S. federal courts have ordered the dismantling of mechanisms which had traditionally been used to separate blacks and whites. The removal of these mechanisms began as early as 1948 when the Supreme Court declared in *Shelly v. Kramer* that racially discriminatory restrictive convenants were not legally enforceable. The effort against discrimination in housing also included the 1968 Fair Housing Law, and the court invoked the federal Civil Rights Act of 1866 which guaranteed to blacks the same rights to inherit, sell, lease, and dispose of property as whites (Barker and Barker 1978).[1]

An additional blow to segregation was dealt in the area of education in 1954 and 1955 with the Brown decisions (*Brown v. Board of Education,* 1954; *Brown v. Board of Education II,* 1955). In a series of decisions following Brown, the courts extended its application.[2] The impact of these decisions was increased by the enactment of the Civil Rights Act of 1964, which precluded giving federal aid to school districts discriminating on the basis of race, and the Elementary and Secondary Education Act (Barker and Barker 1978). The court also rejected dilatory tactics in implementing *Brown.*[3]

The court eventually attacked *de facto* discrimination.[4] Discriminatory practices in northern schools were rejected[5] and busing to achieve racial balance was defended.[6]

The Civil Rights Act of 1964 also prohibited discrimination in the provision of public accommodations. In a number of cases the court upheld the constitutionality of the law.[7] Other court decisions prohibited discrimination in the provision of recreation facilities.[8]

Prior to these policy developments, whites who wished to avoid associating with blacks could do so with little difficulty. The presence of blacks within municipal and school district boundaries was not a consideration of crucial importance because segregative mechanisms minimized white exposure to them. After the Supreme Court removed discriminatory mechanisms, maintaining geographic and, more importantly, social distance (see Berry 1973; Berry et al. 1976; Massey and Mullan 1984; Suttles 1972) became problematic (Baron 1969). If blacks lived in the same school districts as whites, for instance, their children had to be admitted to the same schools as white children.

## Contemporary Developments in Judicial Policy: Bolstering Segregation

Parallel to the dismantling of intra-jurisdictional segregative mechanisms has been the consistent tendency of the federal courts to reinforce the integrity of local jurisdictional boundaries. In *San Antonio Independent School District v. Rodriquez* (1974), the Supreme Court held that disparities in local school district financing did not deny students the equal protection of the laws. In *Milliken v. Bradley* (1974), the court refused to order interdistrict busing absent proof that suburban districts had caused segregation in Detroit's school system. Interdistrict busing programs have been ordered by the court in only two metropolitan areas—Louisville, Kentucky, and Wilmington, Delaware (Orfield 1978; Dimond 1985).

In the area of housing and zoning, the court attacked discriminatory actions in *Hills v. Gautreaux* (1975), and declared that relief in this case might include the entire Chicago Metropolitan Area. In the same case, however, the court asserted that the use of land-use powers by localities to block the development of low-income public housing was not unconstitutional. In a series of cases, the court upheld a California law which required that local voters approve all public housing proposals; upheld the right of localities to engage in restrictive zoning; and imposed a strict standard that zoning prohibiting subsidized housing should be invalidated only if intent to discriminate on racial grounds is proven.[9] A number of other cases have further articulated these stands by the Supreme Court[10] (See Danielson 1976: chapter 7).

The collective significance of these parallel developments is that segregation by various characteristics within jurisdictions is subject to change through legal action; but that segregation at jurisdictional boundaries is relatively secure against legal attack.

What is being suggested here is that overt mechanisms of racial segregation that were used prior to the revolution in civil rights policy have been replaced by new mechanisms. These mechanisms tend to be covert rather than overt, insofar as they exist ostensibly to accomplish purposes other than spatial segregation. They also are *inter*-jurisdictional mechanisms rather than *intra*-jurisdictional mechanisms. Their functioning is supported by, and their effects are manifest at, the formal boundaries of municipalities. As a consequence of this replacement of dismantled discriminatory mechanisms by new ones, patterns of residential segregation are changing.

This change in mechanisms has implications for segregation beyond considerations of race, however. The old, overt mechanisms of discrimination were predicated upon race, racial discrimination being a more or less acceptable goal of policy prior to the 1950s. Since racial discrimination is no longer considered legitimate, segregative mechanisms must be defensible on the grounds that they are meant to accomplish some other purpose. The consequence is that they have a broadened focus, and hence a commensurately broader impact. Segregation is supported now by inter-jurisdictional mechanisms which work on the basis of socioeconomic class rather than race. These mechanisms tend to parse populations along the more encompassing dimension of socioeconomic status, a dimension which often includes, but is not limited to, color.

## Research Design

It is appropriate here to speculate on the likely effect of such a dual trend in public policy. On the one hand, intra-jurisdictional, or what might be termed "neighborhood level" segregative mechanisms have been weakened. On the other hand, segregative mechanisms that are defined by jurisdictional boundaries—for present purposes, "municipal level" mechanisms—have been reinforced. Meanwhile, a persistent influence on residential search activity by whites during this period has been an obdurate aversion to locations which put them in close proximity to blacks (Massey and Mullan 1984; Berry 1973; Danielson 1976; Berry et al. 1976; Palmquist 1984). The removal of certain barriers to minority group movement and the strengthening of other barriers should affect the direction of population flows and, in turn, the destinations at which population groups ultimately arrive. Like water taking the shape of the containers into which it is poured, population flows should conform to changed configurations of discrimination.

To test this hypothesis, data aggregated at the neighborhood and at the municipal levels are examined using analysis of variance. The dependent variables in this analysis are measures of the racial and class composition of neighborhood populations—the proportions of the neighborhood populations comprised by blacks and persons of high socioeconomic status. The question is how much of the variance in these neighborhood proportions is explained by municipal boundaries. The category variable in the analysis of variance, then, is municipality. If the municipal boundaries within which these neighborhoods are subsumed account for a majority of the variance in these proportions, one can conclude that most of the variance that occurs in racial and class attributes of populations occurs among municipalities, not within them. Conversely, if residual variance exceeds the explained variance, then segregation of populations by class and race is a neighborhood phenomenon.

## The Data

Census data will be used to determine if the hypothesized trend in patterns of metropolitan segregation has actually occurred. These data must be aggregated at the two levels of current interest—the municipality and the neighborhood. Census data approximate these levels of aggregation. Data are published by place and by tract in the Standard Metropolitan Statistical Area books of the 1960, 1970 and 1980 decennial censuses of population (U.S. Bureau of the Census, 1983, 1972, 1962) for municipalities with populations of 10,000 or greater. Tracts are imperfect proxies for neighborhoods. The Bureau of the Census tries to make tract boundaries approximate neighborhood boundaries, but the census tract remains a somewhat artificial unit. Nevertheless, the analysis of place and tract data should permit a comparison of population differences within and across jurisdictions.

The places and tracts used in this analysis are taken from Cook County, Illinois, and Los Angeles County, California. These counties were used because no others contained a sufficient number of tracted places in the 1960 census to support statistical analysis. In Cook County in 1960, sixteen places were tracted. Thirty-one places were tracted in Los Angeles County. These places included 141 and 333 census tracts respectively. A number of other metropolitan counties might have been included in the analysis if the 1960 census year were excluded. This would only have provided results for two time points

(1970, 1980), however. Whereas results for three points in time might indicate a trend, results for two points could indicate only a change.

The central cities of these counties, Los Angeles and Chicago, as well as Long Beach, were excluded from analysis. The most important consideration behind this strategy was that these places are so much larger than their suburban municipalities that it was not clear what any results obtained from lumping them together would mean. For instance, the municipalities that are included in the analysis might have five or ten census tracts—one of the very largest might have thirty. Chicago and Los Angeles have hundreds of tracts. Each city has more census tracts within its boundaries than the sum of census tracts within the boundaries of all of the smaller cities examined in either Los Angeles or Cook Counties. If all of these census tracts were introduced into the analysis, the overall number of tracts would treble or quadruple, and the variance in the dependent variable would likely increase proportionately. However, the count of the category variable—municipality—would increase by only one. One would expect the amount of variance explained by the category variable to plummet, but not for any theoretically relevant reason. The reduction in explained variance would simply be an artifact of comparing apples to oranges—or, in this case, a watermelon to lots of grapes.

Furthermore, it is implausible that the difference in size between suburbs and central cities has no impact on the way that persons making locational decisions think about the problem. Suburban municipal boundaries define discrete geographic units which are often readily characterized in socioeconomic terms. Markham (Cook County) is predominately black, Cicero is white and working class, Skokie is heavily Jewish. Settlers with preferences about the ethnic, racial, and class composition of their neighborhoods can relate those preferences immediately to specific geographic units in these cases. If the city of Chicago is substituted, the task of relating preferences to geography becomes much more complex.

Policy which increases the segregative potential of the municipal boundaries of suburbs sharpens their respective socioeconomic identities. It is not possible, however, for such policy to make the socioeconomic identity of Chicago or Los Angeles less amorphous (at least in the short run). In this chapter, attention is limited to outcomes which it is possible for the policy changes that have been discussed to explain. To combine outcomes in central cities and in their suburbs in the analysis would only result in the introduction, again, of variance that the analysis cannot be expected to explain, and the confounding of theoretically different choice situations.

Also excluded were places smaller than 10,000 in population since data comparable to the measures used here are not available for small places. Finally, places were excluded which were not in the central counties (Cook and Los Angeles) of the SMSAs. These two counties are thoroughly urbanized, and it is not too difficult to think that each is subject to a common sorting dynamic. Peripheral counties in SMSAs are not always uniformly urbanized, and they frequently contain ancilliary urban centers which may well generate sorting dynamics of their own.

The analysis is performed on two separate samples of cities for each of the metropolitan counties. In each county, one sample includes all tracted places for each census year. The number of tracted places increases for each county with time, however. The second sample for each county is restricted to the original 1960 cities traced throughout the three census periods. For instance, the analysis was replicated for the sixteen places originally tracted in Cook County in 1960 in the 1970 and 1980 census years. (For convenience of exposition, these originally tracted cities are hereafter referred to as "older cities"). This analysis of a second sample of originally tracted cities is performed to provide rough comparability and to limit the possibility that results are artifactual.

The analysis of variance is performed using three proportional figures for each census tract. These are the proportion of blacks in each population, the proportion of the relevant population that has completed four years of college, and the proportion of the work force which is in professional, managerial, or technical occupations. These particular dependent variables were chosen for two reasons. First, as indicated previously, it is expected that policy changes have had a segregative impact along both race and class dimensions. Second, it was important that the dependent variables include high-resource groups as well as low-resource groups. A great many studies have focused on the extent, methods, and implications of black segregation. Much less has been written about the segregation (or aggregation) of the upper middle class. Because the two are complementary, the latter is of equal significance to the former. Traditional explanations of black segregation, however, shed no light on the process of middle class aggregation. The results of this analysis of variance, given that the dependent variables represent groups that are disparate in their command of resources, suggest a complementary dynamic to traditional minority segregation, and a possible micro-level link between public policy and patterns of residential segregation.

## Results of the Analysis

The proportions of variance explained by municipal boundaries for all tracts and places in each county are presented in Table 4.1.

For all but two measures, the results indicate that the variance explained by municipal boundaries increases monotonically through the three time points. One exception occurs in the variance for the tract proportion of the work force represented by managers and professionals for Cook County. The variance explained by municipal boundaries increases markedly (about fourteen percent) from 1960 to 1970, then decreases somewhat (about 3.5 percent) from 1970 to 1980. Even in this case, however, there is an overall increase of about twelve percent in variance explained.

## Table 4.1. Proportion of Variance Explained by Municipal Boundaries: Cook County, 1960, 1970, 1980, All Places

|  | YEAR | | |
|---|---|---|---|
|  | *1960* | *1970* | *1980* |
| Proportion Black (total variance) | 0.157* (0.0174) | 0.320 (0.0256) | 0.581 (0.0296) |
| Proportion College Educated | 0.580 (0.0201) | 0.696 (0.0194) | 0.698 (0.0252) |
| Proportion Managers and Professionals | 0.456 (0.0339) | 0.603 (0.0200) | 0.574 (0.0239) |
|  | (N = 141) | (N = 204) | (N = 479) |

*F not significant at the 0.0001 level

## Proportion of Variance Explained by Municipal Boundaries: Los Angeles County, 1960, 1970, 1980, All Places

|  | YEAR | | |
|---|---|---|---|
|  | *1960* | *1970* | *1980* |
| Proportion Black (total variance) | 0.344 (0.0198) | 0.554 (0.0300) | 0.691 (0.0403) |
| Proportion College Educated | 0.467 (0.0053) | 0.463 (0.0074) | 0.664 (0.0175) |
| Proportion Managers and Professionals | 0.401 (0.0128) | 0.432 (0.0138) | 0.647 (0.0184) |
|  | (N = 333) | (N = 517) | (N = 671) |

All F significant at the 0.0001 level

The second case is the proportion of tract population which is college-educated for Los Angeles County. From 1960 to 1970, variance explained by municipal boundaries declines 0.0004—in effect, no change at all. From 1970 to 1980, however, the variance explained increases by twenty percent. Again, variance explained increases over the twenty-year period.

Results of the analysis of variance for the older cities in each county are presented in Table 4.2. These results are not substantially different from those reported in Table 4.1. For five of six measures there is a monotonic increase in the variance explained by municipal boundaries.

These results support the hypothesis that the geographic basis of racial and class segregation has changed

### Table 4.2. Proportion of Variance Explained by Municipal Boundaries: Cook County, 1960, 1970, 1980, Original 16 Places

| | YEAR | | |
|---|---|---|---|
| | 1960 | 1970 | 1980 |
| Proportion Black | 0.157* | 0.305 | 0.576 |
| (total variance) | (0.0174) | (0.0313) | (0.0536) |
| Proportion College | 0.580 | 0.680 | 0.765 |
| Educated | (0.0201) | (0.0218) | (0.0310) |
| Proportion Managers | 0.456 | 0.597 | 0.649 |
| and Professionals | (0.0339) | (0.0225) | (0.0267) |
| | (N = 141) | (N = 163) | (N = 172) |

*F not significant at the 0.0001 level

### Proportion of Variance Explained by Municipal Boundaries: Los Angeles County, 1960, 1970, 1980, Original 31 Places

| | YEAR | | |
|---|---|---|---|
| | 1960 | 1970 | 1980 |
| Proportion Black | 0.344 | 0.586 | 0.721 |
| (total variance) | (0.0198) | (0.0334) | (0.0527) |
| Proportion College | 0.467 | 0.451 | 0.559 |
| Educated | (0.0053) | (0.0081) | (0.0146) |
| Proportion Managers | 0.401 | 0.413 | 0.563 |
| and Professionals | (0.0108) | (0.0145) | (0.0164) |
| | (n = 333) | (n = 414) | (n = 434) |

All F significant at the 0.0001 level

in these metropolitan counties. Clearly the geographic segregation of races and socioeconomic groups in 1980 is organized preponderantly by municipal boundaries rather than less formal neighborhood boundaries. Conversely, in 1960 the geographic differentiation of these groups was more a neighborhood-level phenomenon. This pattern of change is consistent with policy developments which have weakened intra-jurisdictional discriminatory mechanisms while reinforcing inter-jurisdictional mechanisms.

### Additional Considerations

Tables 1 and 2 indicate that there is a pattern of increasing total variance over time for the three variables of interest. The only exception to this pattern occurs for tract proportion manager and professional for the two Cook County samples.

This increase in total variance suggests that both internal municipal variance and across-municipal variance may be increasingly simultaneously. In other words, the results leave open the possibility that sorting by race and class has increased at both the neighborhood level and the municipal level.

The results presented in Tables 4.1 and 4.2 produce one conclusion unambiguously. That is, even though the total variance increased, that increase was disproportionately captured by municipal units. This finding is not trivial. In the presence of significant population change, population flows have been channeled predominantly by jurisdictional units, while the ability of neighborhoods to direct them has consistently lessened.

The figures involved here are proportions, however, and they speak to the *relative* importance of the two units. Because the total variance has increased, it is possible that the relative diversity within jurisdictions has decreased while the absolute diversity has increased. In such a case, the heterogeneity of neighborhoods within cities would have increased even while neighborhood boundaries were explaining a smaller proportion of the total variance over time.

To address this second question of absolute variance the change in the total residual variance (as opposed to the residual proportion of the variance) must be examined for the period under consideration. Total residual variance (TRV) figures are presented in Table 4.3. Also presented are the percentage of change in these figures over the twenty-year period. A negative sign indicates a reduction in TRV. In those instances where there has been a reduction in TRV, it is safe to conclude not only that there has been a reduction in the importance of neighborhood sorting relative to municipal sorting; but that there has also been an absolute reduction in the propensity of neighborhood boundaries to sort within cities. These instances are doubly confirmatory of the central hypothesis of this chapter.

## Sorting by Race

The TRVs for the racial variable display three different patterns. First, for the sample of all cities in Cook County, there has been a reduction in residual variance. Neighborhood heterogeneity within sample cities in Cook County has decreased. In Los Angeles County, there is not much change in TRV. For the sample of all cities, there is a small decrease in TRV: for the older cities, there is a somewhat larger increase. Over a period of twenty years, however, these figures do not represent a very significant alteration in the heterogeneity of neighborhoods within cities. On the other hand, there is a substantial increase in TRV for the older cities in Cook County.

It is significant that in both cases in which TRV increased, it was for the older cities in the two counties. These two samples are the ones most likely to contain transitional cities—those which are apparently in transition from all-white to heavily black. These cities are not stably heterogeneous respecting race—they are not in any real sense "integrated." As they are in the process of transition, however, they appear to be integrated if they are examined in cross-section. This temporary appearance of heterogeneity adds to the total variance and the residual variance.

## Table 4.3. Total Variance, Total Explained Variance and Total Residual Variance: Cook County, All Cities

| Proportion Black | *1960* | *1970* | *1980* |
|---|---|---|---|
| Total Variance | 0.0174 | 0.0256 | 0.0296 |
| Explained Variance | 0.0027 | 0.0082 | 0.0172 |
| Residual Variance | 0.0147 | 0.0174 | 0.0124 |
| Percent Change TRV 1960–1980: | | | −15.5 |

| Proportion College Educated | | | |
|---|---|---|---|
| Total Variance | 0.0201 | 0.0194 | 0.0252 |
| Explained Variance | 0.0117 | 0.0135 | 0.0176 |
| Residual Variance | 0.0084 | 0.0059 | 0.0076 |
| Percent Change TRV 1960–1980: | | | −09.8 |

| Proportion Manager and Professional | | | |
|---|---|---|---|
| Total Variance | 0.0339 | 0.0200 | 0.0239 |
| Explained Variance | 0.0155 | 0.0121 | 0.0137 |
| Residual Variance | 0.0184 | 0.0079 | 0.0102 |
| Percent Change TRV 1960–1980: | | | −44.8 |

## Total Variance, Total Explained Variance, and Total Residual Variance: Cook County, Older Cities

| Proportion Black | | | |
|---|---|---|---|
| Total Variance | 0.0174 | 0.0313 | 0.0536 |
| Explained Variance | 0.0027 | 0.0095 | 0.0309 |
| Residual Variance | 0.0147 | 0.0217 | 0.0227 |
| Percent Change TRV 1960–1980: | | | +35.4 |

| Proportion College Educated | | | |
|---|---|---|---|
| Total Variance | 0.0201 | 0.0218 | 0.0310 |
| Explained Variance | 0.0117 | 0.0148 | 0.0237 |
| Residual Variance | 0.0084 | 0.0070 | 0.0073 |
| Percent Change TRV 1960–1980: | | | −13.7 |

| Proportion Manager and Professional | | | |
|---|---|---|---|
| Total Variance | 0.0339 | 0.0225 | 0.0267 |
| Explained Variance | 0.0155 | 0.0134 | 0.0173 |

**Table 4.3** *(Continued)*

| Residual Variance | 0.0184 | 0.0091 | 0.0094 |
|---|---|---|---|
| Percent Change TRV 1960–1980: | | | −49.2 |

## Total Variance, Total Explained Variance, Total Residual Variance: Los Angeles County, All Places

| Proportion Black | 1960 | 1970 | 1980 |
|---|---|---|---|
| Total Variance | 0.0198 | 0.0300 | 0.0403 |
| Explained Variance | 0.0068 | 0.0166 | 0.0278 |
| Residual Variance | 0.0130 | 0.0134 | 0.0124 |
| Percent Change TRV 1960–1980: | | | −04.2 |

| Proportion College Educated | | | |
|---|---|---|---|
| Total Variance | 0.0053 | 0.0074 | 0.0175 |
| Explained Variance | 0.0025 | 0.0034 | 0.0116 |
| Residual Variance | 0.0028 | 0.0040 | 0.0059 |
| Percent Change TRV 1960–1980: | | | +108.5 |

| Proportion Manager or Professional | | | |
|---|---|---|---|
| Total Variance | 0.0128 | 0.0138 | 0.0184 |
| Explained Variance | 0.0051 | 0.0060 | 0.0119 |
| Residual Variance | 0.0077 | 0.0078 | 0.0065 |
| Percent Change TRV 1960–1980: | | | −15.4 |

## Total Variance, Total Explained Variance, Total Residual Variance: Los Angeles County, Older Cities

| Proportion Black | | | |
|---|---|---|---|
| Total Variance | 0.0198 | 0.0334 | 0.0515 |
| Explained Variance | 0.0068 | 0.0196 | 0.0372 |
| Residual Variance | 0.0130 | 0.0138 | 0.0143 |
| Percent Change TRV 1960–1980: | | | +08.9 |

| Proportion College Educated | | | |
|---|---|---|---|
| Total Variance | 0.0053 | 0.0081 | 0.0168 |
| Explained Variance | 0.0025 | 0.0036 | 0.0094 |
| Residual Variance | 0.0028 | 0.0044 | 0.0074 |
| Percent Change TRV 1960–1980: | | | +164.8 |

**Table 4.3.** *(Continued)*

Proportion Manager or
Professional

| | | | |
|---|---|---|---|
| Total Variance | 0.0108 | 0.0145 | 0.0165 |
| Explained Variance | 0.0043 | 0.0060 | 0.0093 |
| Residual Variance | 0.0065 | 0.0085 | 0.0072 |
| Percent Change TRV 1960–1980: | | | +11.1 |

The argument that these cities are transitional rests upon extensive research by social scientists. A number of them posit the existence of a "tipping-point" (Schelling 1978; Grodzins 1957; Steinnes 1972). They argue that once a geographic unit has experienced a substantial penetration by blacks, it is very unlikely that it will continue to attract white residents (e.g. Duncan and Duncan 1957; Berry et al. 1976).

Following this theory, the analysis of variance for the respective samples is replicated after deleting transitional cities. Transitional cities are taken to be those which have gone from being all white, or nearly so, to having experienced significant black penetration over the twenty-year period. Any city which in 1960 was less than five percent black but exhibited an increase of ten percentage points or more by 1980 has been deleted. The results of the additional analysis are presented in Table 4.4.

In the absence of the transitional cities, the residual variance in the racial variable is reduced significantly for all four samples. Not only were municipal units becoming more efficient as sorting mechanisms from 1960 through 1980, but they were becoming more homogeneous internally with respect to race. The exception to this rule is provided by the transitional cities which, however, give only the appearance of integration as their populations undergo substantial compositional change.

*Segregation by Educational Achievement*

Again, the TRVs for the educational variable follow three patterns over time (Table 4.3). Among the older cit-

## Table 4.4. Proportion of Variance Explained by Municipal Boundaries: Cook County, 1960, 1970, 1980, Transitional Cities Deleted

|  | YEAR | | |
| --- | --- | --- | --- |
| Proportion Black | *1960* | *1970* | *1980* |
| Variance Explained | 0.154* | 0.329 | 0.570 |
| Total Variance | 0.0205 | 0.0253 | 0.0251 |
| Residual Variance | 0.0173 | 0.0170 | 0.0108 |
| Change TRV: 1960–1980 | | | −37.8% |
| | (N = 115) | (N = 175) | (N = 456) |

## Proportion of Variance Explained by Municipal Boundaries, Cook County, 1960, 1970, 1980, Original 16 Places, Transitional Cities Deleted

| | | | |
| --- | --- | --- | --- |
| Variance Explained | 0.154* | 0.313 | 0.582 |
| Total Variance | 0.0205 | 0.0323 | 0.0473 |
| Residual Variance | 0.0173 | 0.0222 | 0.0141 |
| Change TRV: 1960–1980 | | | −18.4% |
| | (N = 352) | (N = 543) | (N = 747) |

## Proportion of Variance Explained by Municipal Boundaries: Los Angeles County, 1960, 1970, 1980, Transitional Cities Deleted

| | | | |
| --- | --- | --- | --- |
| Variance Explained | 0.340* | 0.622 | 0.732 |
| Total Variance | 0.0232 | 0.0502 | 0.0427 |
| Residual Variance | 0.0153 | 0.0190 | 0.0114 |
| Change TRV: 1960–1980 | | | −25.3% |
| | (N = 115) | (N = 134) | (N = 142) |

## Proportion of Variance Explained by Municipal Boundaries: Los Angeles County, 1960, 1970, 1980, Original 31 Places, Transitional Cities Deleted

| | | | |
| --- | --- | --- | --- |
| Variance Explained | 0.340* | 0.669 | 0.803 |
| Total Variance | 0.0232 | 0.0337 | 0.0409 |
| Residual Variance | 0.0153 | 0.0111 | 0.0080 |
| Change TRV: 1960–1980 | | | −47.4% |
| | (N = 352) | (N = 351) | (N = 375) |

*Not significant at the 0.0001 level

ies in Cook County, there is a slight reduction in residual variance. Among the cities in the larger Cook County sample, the reduction is smaller and probably signifies little real change. For both of the Los Angeles County samples, however, the increase in residual variance in the tract proportion of the population completing college is dramatic. There is no obvious explanation for this marked difference between Cook County and Los Angeles County.

## Segregation by Occupation

In three of these four samples, total residual variance has decreased from 1960 to 1980 (Table 4.3). In the fourth, there is a slight increase. This increase occurs among the older cities in Los Angeles County. The increase is not large given the twenty year expanse of the interval. Explained variance in the occupational variable increased by 115% over the same period. With one exception, sampled cities became less heterogeneous internally with respect to the geographic distribution of high status occupational groups; and the sorting process for all cities came to be principally mediated by municipalities rather than neighborhoods.

## The Link Between Policy and
## Inter-Jurisdictional Segregation

This chapter argues that the failure of policy to ameliorate residential segregation is ultimately explained by the continuing desire of whites to avoid areas of heavy black residential concentration. This micro-level structure of preferences is possibly what connects changes in policy with the changes in the geographic organization of segregation discussed here.

This argument hinges on reasoning about the decision-making calculus of individuals making locational decisions. Since direct evidence at the individual level that this decision process is actually used by some number of such settlers has not been produced, the argument is only speculative. One solution would be to provide survey data indicating that settlers frequently refer to municipal boundaries as a source of information in housing market searches. Existing surveys which attempt to isolate the role of information in such searches, however, have proven inconclusive (Smith and Clark 1980). Unfortunately, such surveys do not address the way in which settlers define "distinct subareas, each of which is relatively homogeneous with respect to the chance of finding an acceptable vacancy" (Smith and Clark 1980: 108).

*Exclusion, Recruitment, and Resources*

Exclusion has been frequently offered as an explanation for the residential concentration of blacks and low-income groups (Danielson 1976; Frieden 1979). Miller (1981) documents the use of exclusionary powers to isolate blacks in Los Angeles County. Logan and Schneider (1984) find that blacks in suburbia tend to be concentrated in places with weak tax bases and high tax rates. "It is not plausible to argue that blacks are more attracted to such places . . . ," they write. Rather, they conclude that "this finding indicates that the dual housing market effectively steers blacks to disadvantaged communities" (Logan and Schneider 1984: 886–887).

However, if exclusion is invoked to explain the pattern of black increases, it cannot also be invoked to explain patterns of settlement by the college educated, managers, and professionals. Exclusionary powers operate on differences in the distribution of resources. Groups that are excluded are inherently low-resource groups. The plausibility of the exclusionary explanation regarding blacks arises from the fact that a disproportionate number of blacks have few resources. This is not true, however, of the college-educated and the well-employed. Once exclusion is used to explain the concentration of low-resource populations in certain municipalities, the question remains: How do high-resource persons arrive in other municipalities? This is a question, not of exclusion, but of what might better be called recruitment ("places competing for people," Molotch 1972), and, in answering this question, one needs to focus on the identities of places, the preferences of high-resource settlers, and the sources of the information that they use to match places and preferences.

Exclusion can explain something about the geographic distribution of low-resource groups. It does so by revealing the ways in which the choices of these groups are limited. But the choices of groups that have resources are not limited by exclusionary mechanisms. There is a fundamental asymmetry in the metropolitan sorting dynamic, then, between what might be called "choice-makers" and "choice-takers." The choice-takers are those who face barriers of exclusion. They take choices that are imposed upon them by other actors. High-resource groups, however, are relatively free to make their own choices. If one wishes to explain sorting as it is manifested among these groups, one must explain choices rather than constraints.

The perception of this asymmetric choice dynamic with respect to resources was one of the reasons for choosing the dimensions of segregation—race, college education, high status occupation—that are examined here. High-status communities may employ political autonomy to exclude low-status persons, but such exclusion clearly represents only part of the sorting dynamic. If high-status do nothing but exclude "undesirables", they must eventually disappear through attrition. How do they replace highly educated, prestigiously employed members of upper and upper middle classes who die or move away? This question, as well as the results of the analysis of variance which indicate increasing homogeneity among high as well as low-resource populations by municipality, suggest that it is important to think about the factors which structure the location decisions of high-resource persons.

*Boundaries, Information, and Information Costs*

Attention must be given to the critical role of information when considering the choices of high-resource persons engaged in housing market searches (Smith and Clark 1980). When attempting to realize preferences about locations, settlers require information about the characteristics of the alternatives from which they are likely to choose. Those engaged in housing market searches face formidable limitations of time and information (Smith and Clark 1980). Information costs and the reliability of various sources of information must play a substantial role in determining which sources of information settlers choose, and, in turn, the locations at which they ultimately arrive.

The policy developments which have been traced early in this chapter give added impetus to the exclusionary dynamic. Additionally, however, it can be argued that they increase the reliability of the information that is offered to settlers by municipal boundaries. In doing so, they cause persons engaged in housing market search to turn to a source of information that is considerably less costly than the information generated by and about neighborhoods.

Municipal boundaries provide information to persons choosing among prospective locations. Considered in itself, this statement is trivially true. But there are a number of other sources of information available to settlers. Which of these sources of information is most influential?

Urban political boundaries not only provide information, but settlers incur smaller costs in availing themselves of that information. The boundaries of urban jurisdictions are highly visible. In contrast, neighborhood boundaries are comparatively poor sources of information because boundaries of neighborhoods are not precisely defined. No external agency that residents recognize as authoritative establishes the bounds of neighborhoods. Hence, neighborhood definition is a matter of the perceptions of individual residents (Downs 1981: 13).

The research which indicates that neighborhoods are not clearly visible or objectively defined in the cognitions of residents has been recounted at other points in this book (chapter 2). In spite of the strong intuition that there must be natural areas within cities (Park 1952; Suttles 1972), sociological research reveals a great deal of ambiguity in the minds of city dwellers about the exact location of neighborhood boundaries (Hunter 1975; Molotch 1972; Form et al. 1954; Downs 1981). The advantage of political boundaries is that they precisely define the geographic component of place.

In short, though it is recognized that there are distinctive neighborhoods in cities, their names, boundaries, and socioeconomic characters are not easily determined. One imagines, then, that the cues provided to settlers are ambiguous. By comparison, urban political boundaries are quite accessible, and their potential for conveying information substantially greater.

## Political Boundaries and Future Conditions

A second argument regarding urban political boundaries is that policy developments over a period of forty years have made them more reliable predictors of future life conditions in a given location. The value of boundaries as sources of information results precisely from the fact that Congress and the federal courts have dismantled many of the intra-jurisdictional sorting mechanisms that formerly structured segregation within political units. One can suppose that some settlers move into subareas in order to be isolated from types of persons that they find undesirable. They can better expect to remain isolated from such persons if they move into a political jurisdiction—a municipality—than they could if they moved into a similarly desirable neighborhood. Metropolitan governmental fragmentation and the federal judiciary's respect for local autonomy provide settlers with the incentive to seek out towns—rather than congenial *neighborhoods*—that comply with their preferences. Downs speaks of the pressure that leads middle class households to opt for incorporation so that "socioeconomic segregation can be achieved through legal means, rather than just market forces" (1981: 49). It is reasonable to think that the desire to give legal sanction to socioeconomic segregation also affects the decision-making calculus of persons choosing locations. The political boundary provides a more convincing barrier to invasion by intruder groups than does an intangible and ambiguous neighborhood boundary.

The point of this discussion is that policy developments, which have eliminated some segregative mechanisms while reaffirming the use of others, are linked to a shift in segregation from the neighborhood to the jurisdicitional level in two ways. The first is that they reinforce and encourage the use of exclusionary powers on the part of predominantly white, high-resource municipalities. The second is that they have changed the nature of the information available to persons making location decisions. Such persons are now able to identify relatively homogeneous geographic units having racial and socioeconomic characteristics, and thus a determinate place identity, which reflect their preferences at relatively low information cost; and they have better assurances that these units will retain their place identity into the future.

## Conclusion

This chapter identifies two parallel developments in American public policy. One is the dismantling of intra-jurisdictional mechanisms which in the past sorted populations on racial characteristics. The second is the reaffirmation of municipal powers which tend to segregate racial and socioeconomic groups inter-jurisdictionally. The central hypothesis of this chapter is that this change in the geographic incidence of segregative mechanisms should result in a change in geographic patterns of segregation. Tract and municipal level census data from Los Angeles and Cook Counties indicate that such a shift has, in fact, taken place. In these counties, segregation by race, educational attainment, and occupation has come to be organized by city rather than neighborhood over the period 1960–1980.

This chapter suggests that policy changes are linked to changes in patterns of segregation by processes of exclusion and recruitment. Under the former, low-resource individuals—blacks, the poorly educated, those in lower status occupations—are excluded from higher status municipalities through the use of controls over zoning, construction, and so on. The recruitment process operates on high-resource individuals through an increasing tendency for information about locations to be structured by municipal boundaries.

This work suggests an obvious area for future research. More data are needed which can provide insight into the way in which locational decisions are made. Surveys are needed which are designed to address the processes by which persons making housing market searches define discrete geographic units—those "homogeneous subareas" in which they can expect to find "acceptable vacancies." Such surveys will increase our ability to identify linkages between public policy and patterns of residential segregation.

## Notes

1. *Jones v. Mayer,* 1968.

2. *Bolling v. Sharpe,* 1954; *Cooper v. Aaron, 1958; Griffin v. Prince Edward County School Board,* 1964; *Rogers v. Paul,* 1965.

3. *United States v. Jefferson County Board of Education* 1966; *Alexander v. Holmes County Board of Education,* 1969.

4. *Hobsen v. Hansen* 1967.

5. *Keyes v. School District No. 1, Denver, Colorado,* 1973.

6. *Swann v. Charlotte Mechklenburg Board of Education,* 1971; *North Carolina State Board of Education v. Swann,* 1971.

7. *Heart of Atlanta Motel v. United States* (1964); *Katzenbach v. McClung,* 1964; *United States v. Northwest Louisiana Restaurant Club,* 1966.

8. *Muir v. Louisville Park Theatrical Association,* 1954; *Simkins v. City of Greensboro,* 1957; *Gilmore v. City of Montgomery, Alabama,* 1974.

9. *James v. Valtierra,* 1971; *Village of Belle Terre v. Borass,* 1974; *Arlington Heights v. Metropolitan Housing Development Corporation,* 1977.

10. *Avecedo v. Nassau County, New York,* 1974; *Ybarra v. Town of Los Altos Hills,* 1973; *Mahaley v. Cuyahoga Metropolitan Housing Authority,* 1976; see Danielson 1976: chapter 7 and notes.

# 5

# *The Impact of*
# *Boundary Configuration*

Congruent boundaries should sort more effectively than cross-cutting boundaries which define overlapping jurisdictions. The basis of this argument is the contention that there is a layering of functions that occurs when boundaries of various jurisdictions coincide. The primary function of a formal boundary is to demarcate one place from another. When the boundary describes the "metes and bounds" of a municipality, it also indicates the geographic area within which certain services can be had at a certain cost. The boundary is also associated with a population of determinate demographic and socioeconomic composition. When municipal boundaries follow school district boundaries, an additional layering of functions occurs. More services and costs are united with a discrete geography; and the accompanying population can be expected to influence the associations and relationships of children in schools and of family members in neighborhoods.

Each additional function that is placed upon a political boundary increases the amount of information that the boundary conveys. The amount of information thus carried by boundaries can be substantial. It can include information about physical aspects of the natural and built environments, about an array of services and taxes, about types of social interaction, and generally about the quality of life and life style associated with a particular location.

When a large number of functions are layered on a single political boundary, place identity is more clearly defined, and a great deal of information becomes available at relatively low cost to individuals making locational decisions. Under these circumstances, it is easier for such persons to determine the characteristics of a prospective location. Individuals who value the characteristics of the spatial unit described by a boundary will be attracted to it. Others who find these characteristics distasteful will seek locations elsewhere. In sum, when boundaries carry a good deal of information, sorting will occur with relatively high efficiency on the basis of characteristics salient to large groups of settlers.

By implication, when boundaries cross and jurisdictions overlap, the efficiency of boundaries as sorting mechanisms should be impaired. A municipality may be divided, for instance, among two or more school districts. One may suppose that a family looking for a house is interested both in the quality of life in their residential location and the quality of education in schools. If they seek housing in the educationally divided municipality, their locational decision is split—they must decide not only to locate within the municipality, but within a particular school district within the municipality. The cues given by the municipal boundary in this situation are responsive to only a subset of the individual's preferences respecting locations. In cases such as these, the sorting done by municipal boundaries is confounded with sorting done by school district boundaries.

The empirical implications of the theory in this area are straightforward. When boundaries coincide and cues are relatively unambiguous, the populations of the spatial units involved should be internally homogeneous. When boundaries cross and there is little coincidence of jurisdictions of various kinds, the result should be heterogeneity within jurisdictional populations. We turn to cases in St. Louis county.

## Municipalities in St. Louis County

This analysis relies upon an examination of forty-six municipalities in St. Louis County, Missouri. These are the forty-six cities in the county for which data are published in the 1980 Census of Population and Housing (Bureau of the Census 1983c). They range in population from just over 2,500 to 55,372 (St. Louis County Department of Planning 1982). Eighteen of these cities exceed 10,000 in population. The remaining twenty-eight cities have populations between 2,500 and 10,000. Eight of these municipalities are split between two or more school districts, while 38 are wholly contained within a single district. Basic statistics for these 46 cities are presented in Table 5.1.

Some of the theoretical considerations in favor of focusing on this group of cities have been previously discussed. St. Louis County lies within a prototypical metropolitan area, constituting (together with the City of St. Louis) the heart of the nation's twelfth largest SMSA (St. Louis County Department of Planning 1982). Like most metropolitan areas St. Louis County is jurisdictionally fragmented. It encompasses 286 service districts including 90 municipalities, 24 school districts, and an assortment of street-lighting districts, sewer districts, library districts, junior college districts, fire protection districts, regional development districts, and so on (St. Louis County Department of Planning 1982: 119–120). Of these, 193 are empowered to tax (St. Louis County Department of Planning 1982). Municipalities in St. Louis County are near enough to the metropolitan center and have sufficient population density to fall within regional dynamics of economic and social differentiation (Meade 1972).

The logistics of the research situation are as important as these theoretical qualifications. Data on the relationships of local boundaries to each other are not always readily available. Even for governments of urbanized counties with large, professional staffs it is rarely the responsibility of any one agency to collect and publish information about the spatial overlap of jurisdictions. One

## Table 5.l. Unified and Split Municipalities: Basic Data

| Unified Municipalities | Incor- porated | Area (Sq. Mi.) | Popula- tion | Assessed Val. (thousands) |
|---|---|---|---|---|
| Ballwin | 1950 | 4.028 | 12,656 | 55,407 |
| Bel Ridge | 1947 | 0.767 | 3,682 | 7,403 |
| Bellefontaine | 1950 | 4.292 | 12,082 | 36,423 |
| Berkeley | 1937 | 4.869 | 16,146 | 79,977 |
| Black Jack | 1970 | 2.581 | 5,293 | 17,738 |
| Breckenridge Hills | 1950 | 0.798 | 5,666 | 12,047 |
| Brentwood | 1919 | 2.158 | 8,209 | 45,969 |
| Clayton | 1913 | 2.541 | 14,219 | 119,201 |
| Crestwood | 1947 | 3.148 | 12,815 | 55,991 |
| Ellisville | 1932 | 3.505 | 6,233 | 37,083 |
| Eureka | 1954 | 6.867 | 3,862 | 16,927 |
| Ferguson | 1894 | 6.234 | 24,740 | 74,807 |
| Frontenac | 1947 | 2.895 | 3,654 | 37,589 |
| Glendale | 1912 | 1.317 | 6,035 | 22,295 |
| Hazelwood | 1949 | 4.861 | 12,935 | 97,001 |
| Jennings | 1946 | 3.781 | 17,026 | 50,545 |
| Kinloch | 1948 | 0.719 | 4,455 | 5,436 |
| Kirkwood | 1865 | 8.919 | 27,987 | 105,821 |
| Ladue | 1936 | 8.566 | 9,376 | 84,981 |
| Manchester | 1950 | 2.119 | 6,191 | 28,388 |
| Maplewood | 1908 | 1.553 | 10,960 | 35,543 |
| Moline Acres | 1949 | 0.566 | 2,774 | 8,473 |
| Normandy | 1945 | 1.859 | 5,174 | 13,717 |
| Northwoods | 1939 | 0.680 | 5,831 | 13,395 |
| Olivette | 1930 | 2.775 | 8,039 | 43,828 |
| Overland | 1939 | 4.388 | 19,620 | 64,922 |
| Pagedale | 1950 | 1.094 | 4,542 | 15,115 |
| Pine Lawn | 1947 | 0.625 | 6,662 | 9,155 |
| Riverview | 1950 | 0.811 | 3,367 | 9,361 |
| Rock Hill | 1929 | 1.075 | 5,702 | 17,793 |
| St. John | 1945 | 1.417 | 7,854 | 20,009 |
| Sunset Hills | 1957 | 6.216 | 4,363 | 37,553 |
| Town and Country | 1950 | 4.181 | 3,187 | 32,734 |
| University City | 1906 | 5.859 | 42,738 | 119,602 |
| Valley Park | 1917 | 2.302 | 3,232 | 10,818 |
| Webster Groves | 1896 | 5.789 | 23,097 | 77,820 |
| Wellston | 1949 | 0.922 | 4,495 | 12,855 |
| Woodson Terrace | 1946 | 0.813 | 4,798 | 15,796 |

**Table 5.1.** *(Continued)*

Split Municipalities:

| | | | | |
|---|---|---|---|---|
| Bridgeton | 1843 | 14.933 | 18,445 | 114,267 |
| Creve Coeur | 1949 | 7.522 | 11,757 | 130,262 |
| Dellwood | 1951 | 1.041 | 6,200 | 15,748 |
| Des Peres | 1934 | 4.152 | 8,254 | 63,317 |
| Florissant | 1857 | 9.970 | 55,372 | 147,840 |
| Richmond Heights | 1913 | 2.353 | 11,516 | 54,814 |
| St. Ann | 1948 | 3.128 | 15,523 | 50,546 |
| Shrewsbury | 1913 | 1.416 | 5,077 | 18,990 |

agency may have information about municipalities, or about school districts, or about special districts of various kinds. In all probability, however, no agency will be charged with routinely producing documents that indicate which municipalities are in which school districts, which school districts are split between municipalities, which are coterminous with municipalities, and so on. When such information exists, it frequently requires the examination of a variety of publications, comparisons of a number of maps, and conversations with county officials, city clerks, and school superintendents to pull it all together. In less urbanized counties on the outskirts of SMSAs, the success of the endeavor is greatly in doubt.

One way of avoiding these problems is to concentrate on a limited number of jurisdictions for which information is reasonably accessible. The forty-six municipalities in St. Louis County constitute a sample of manageable proportions. A substantial store of information about these municipalities is available due to the prodigious efforts of the St. Louis County Department of Planning, in particular the Office of Research and Statistics. In those cases in which information is required in greater detail, it is not unreasonable to examine individual cases. Data on single municipalities are available from local libraries and city officials.

Of course, limiting the number of cases in this way impugns the generality of any conclusions that may result. There is a partial check against this loss of generalizability insofar as St. Louis County is typical of fragmented urban areas. There are no obvious reasons to suppose that fragmentation in Cook County or Wayne County or Los Angeles County or San Mateo County (Orlebeke 1983; Mowitz and Wright 1962; Miller 1981; Scott and Corzine 1971) is different than fragmentation in St. Louis County. Nevertheless, the applicability of the findings of this chapter beyond St. Louis County remains to be demonstrated.

### Unified and Split Municipalities and Recruitment

The chief theoretical argument in favor of this sample of municipalities is that it provides examples of two different boundary configurations. These two groups of municipalities—those which are split by school district boundaries and those which are not—can be compared to see if there are notable differences in the sorting efficiency of their boundaries. Theory predicts that the boundaries of the unified municipalities will sort more effectively.

This comparison should cast some light on the degree to which political boundaries actually support recruitment. The reason is that school district boundaries are not fortified with exclusionary powers. School boards do not make zoning decisions nor promulgate construction codes. The sorting that takes place across a school district boundary must be supported by the information that resides there. If it is found that school district boundaries structure detectable differences within municipal populations, there will be a strong suggestion that these differences are the result of differential recruitment. It is not always possible to reach such a conclusion about sorting across municipal boundaries because of the confounding of exclusionary sorting and recruitment.

By the theory of sorting at boundaries previously articulated, sorting should be least efficient when boundaries cross and jurisdictions overlap. Therefore, one of the factors which should help in understanding differences in sorting across municipal boundaries is their relationship to the boundaries of other jurisdictions. In St. Louis County, the cases of municipalities that are split between school districts offer themselves for examination. The advantage of focusing on these cases is that if it is found that they are more heterogeneous than municipalities that are not divided, this finding is *prima facie* evidence that sorting based on information does occur across political boundaries. This is sorting by recruitment rather than exclusion because it is sorting that occurs *within* exclusionary boundaries and across a boundary that has only an information function. If there are differences within municipal populations that are structured by school district boundaries, it must be because the school districts have recruited different types of people.

## The Problem of Comparing Jurisdictions

At this point, the problem is to generate measures of population eccentricity. A preliminary question is "What should be measured?" Of what does one speak in referring to eccentricity? Sociologists commonly discuss spatial differentiation of populations along a number of dimensions. Some of these dimensions have been the basis of previous references to characteristics that are "salient" to persons making locational decisions. One of these dimensions is race (Massey and Mullan 1984; Molotch 1971; Duncan and Duncan 1957; Taeuber and Taeuber 1965; Palmquist 1984). Only slightly less prominent have been studies of spatial segregation by socioeconomic status (Anderson and Egelund 1961; Duncan and Duncan 1955a; Feldman and Tilly 1966; Guest 1971; Schnore 1972; Eklund and Williams 1978; Lauman 1966; Stein 1987). Socioeconomic status is usually measured in these studies in terms of income, education, or occupational status, or some composite measure of the three. There has also been some examination of differentiation by family structure (Anderson and Egelund 1961; Shevky and Bell 1955; Hunter 1975). Indeed, a number of ecological analyses have found that family structure is one of the most fundamental bases of differentiation. These are the substantive dimensions of differentiation that have been used in the following analyses both because there is some theoretical precedent and because data on these characteristics are readily available in the census.

The next problem is to determine how one can know if there are differences between unified and split municipalities in terms of the eccentricity of their populations along the dimensions here discussed.

Boundaries of unified municipalities should sort more effectively than the boundaries of municipalities that are split between two or more school districts. The evidence of this more effective sorting takes the form of greater eccentricity along salient dimensions in the populations of unified municipalities. After all, if one says that a boundary sorts "more effectively" she must mean that it is good at selecting persons of a particular type and rejecting others. This being the case, it must be true that the population within the boundary becomes eccentric in that it differs from others by having a noticeably higher concentration of persons with certain characteristics.

What is meant, then, by saying that the boundaries of unified municipalities sort more effectively is that these municipalities should fall at the extremes of various distributions. If the characteristic in question were race, for instance, the expectation would be that unified municipalities would be more nearly all black or all white. Split municipalities, conversely, should be less racially distinctive.

The question, then, is whether there is greater spatial segregation of persons by certain characteristics among unified municipalities than there is among split municipalities. A statistic that would express the degree of spatial segregation by race, class, family structure, and so on among some group of municipalities would serve present purposes. It might be computed for both split and unified municipalities and the values for the two groups could then be compared. There would then be some reason to conclude that one type of municipality is more eccentric on average than the other.

## The Index of Dissimilarity

An intense campaign to determine an appropriate statistical measure of spatial segregation was conducted from 1947 to 1955 (Winship 1977; Lieberson and Carter 1982; Massey and Denton 1988b). From these battles, the Index of Dissimilarity (D) developed by Duncan and Duncan (1955a) emerged. It has been used heavily because of its ease of computation and its straightforward substantive interpretation.

The index of dissimilarity is computed using the formula

$$(1) \quad D = \frac{\sum_{i=1}^{n} T_i |P_i - P|}{2TP(1-P)}$$

The real work is done by the numerator of the right hand term of the equation, a weighted sum of the populations ($T_i$) of the spatial units that comprise the spatial aggregate for which D is to be computed. The various i units in the spatial aggregate might, for instance, be the census tracts that make up a city, or, as with present cases, the municipalities that are located in an urban county. Each population is weighted by the factor $P_i - P$, the difference between the proportion of the population in the ith unit bearing the relevant characteristic and the overall proportion of the spatial aggregate bearing the same characteristic. Two things, then, determine the size of this numerator and hence the magnitude of D: (1) the extent to which spatial units have eccentric proportional values relative to the overall proportion of the larger unit; and (2) the size of the unit population to be weighted by a given proportional difference. D *is* actually a measure of the eccentricity of spatial units as eccentricity has previously been defined (chapter 1).

The numerator on the right side of equation 1 represents the number of persons in the aggregate unit that must move to achieve perfect integration ($P_i = P$ for all i). The denominator gives the number that would have to move to achieve perfect integration of the aggregate unit if spatial segregation were complete. Their ratio (D) is the proportion of the population of the aggregate unit that must move to bring about complete spatial integration (Winship 1977; White 1983; Morgan 1983; Massey and Denton 1988b).

Recently, however, there has been more strife in the literature over the appropriateness of D as a measure of spatial segregation in diverse applications (White 1983; Morgan 1983; Lieberson and Carter 1982; Winship 1977, 1978; Falk, Cortese, and Cohen 1978; Massey 1978; Kestenbaum 1980; Logan and Stearns 1986; Schnare 1980; Massey and Denton 1988b). Many of these criticisms serve only to reveal that there are a number of dimensions of segregation (Massey and Denton 1988b) and that the index of dissimilarity does not account for all of them. D has its shortcomings in that it is insensitive to the distances between and the clustering of groups (White 1983; Morgan 1983) and to the likelihood that members of one group will come into contact with members of the other (Lieberson and Carter 1982). The literature would indicate then, that there has been widespread dissatisfaction with D in recent years, and that a number of alternates have been proposed to remedy this or that deficiency. It seems clear, however, that no replacement for D has been found that doesn't have serious shortcomings of its own.

In truth, D's near absolute victory over its competitors in the 1950s and its predominance for the next twenty years was probably unwarranted. During the period that the initial battle was raging, there was an understanding "that there were many different indexes, each of which was appropriate for different theoretical reasons" (Winship 1977: 1058). It might be wise to revive something of this attitude for contemporary use. In particular, one cannot expect that D will capture in a single number everything that is meant when one says "segregation". Nor should anyone expect that some other such superstatistic is on the horizon. Statistics should, rather, be chosen with an eye to their limitations and to theoretical requirements. The question under consideration is one of blunt spatial segregation across units, or what Massey and Denton (1988b) refer to as "evenness", and insensitivity to these other shadings of segregation does not invalidate the index of dissimilarity for these purposes. Massey and Denton have shown that D is an appropriate measure of evenness, and that, among all possible measures of this dimension of segregation, it is in many ways the most desirable. What is needed in this chapter is a summary measure of the eccentricity of different types of municipalities. All in all, D, modified for comparative purposes, appears an appropriate choice.

## Initial Comparison

Other criticisms are not so easily dismissed. It has been demonstrated that the value of D is dependent upon the proportion black (or poor, or college-educated, or white collar workers) of the unit under consideration. In the present application, these units are the two groups of municipalities in St. Louis County. If the overall proportion black, etc., among unified municipalities differs much from the proportion black among split municipalities, the comparison of D values for the two groups will be impaired. The problem is that, all other things being equal, "the smaller the proportion of the population belonging to the minority, the larger the expected value of the index" (White 1983: 1010; Winship 1977: 1062).

The split municipalities have smaller proportional values on the race, occupation, and education dimensions than the unified municipalities. The resulting distortion of D, then, might be expected to preclude meaningful comparison. Interestingly enough, when D is computed for each dimension by group using overall group proportions, it is the group of unified municipalities that has the higher values (0.580, 0.260, and 0.376 compared to 0.380, 0.221, and 0.312 for race, occupation, and education respectively). If anything the differences between unified and split municipalities are even greater than these computations would indicate.

On the other hand, the split municipality group has a greater value for spatial segregation by family structure than the unified municipality group (0.164 to 0.126). Since the proportion of households comprised by traditional families is larger for the split municipalities than the unified municipalities, one can conclude that, if anything, the D valued for unified municipalities is artificially inflated. Consequently, and contrary to expectations, it is safe to assert that the split municipalities are more eccentric regarding the family structure of their populations than the unified municipalities; indeed, that they are even more eccentric relatively than is indicated by these D values.

Three out of four is not bad, however, and because the question is more the polarity of relationships between the two groups of cities than a precise determination of the magnitude of these differences, these results can be taken as a qualified confirmation of the previous claim about the impact of boundary configuration. For three out of four dimensions for which the index of dissimilarity was calculated, the indication is that greater spatial segregation exists on average among unified municipalities than among split municipalities. Any distortion of effects owing to differences in the sizes of aggregate proportions of the two groups is in favor of the theory. That is, if anything, these differences are not only in the right direction, but more substantial than the ones reported. Comparability of the results obtained for each of the two groups of cities, therefore, is not an issue.


## Modifying D For Comparative Applications

Comparing unified and split municipalities in this fashion is not completely satisfying, however. It might be adequate if the concern were for spatial segregation in separate SMSAs. Metropolitan areas are natural aggregates and it makes intuitive sense to compare them. The comparison of a group of unified municipalities and a group of split municipalities, all of which are located in the same metropolitan county, is not so intuitively convincing. How should one interpret the fact that one group is less segregated internally than the other?

The problem is that levels of spatial segregation in each group of municipalities are internally calculated using overall proportions that have no meaning outside of their respective aggregates. Suppose that the aggregate proportion of college graduates in the unified municipalities is 0.300, while the aggregate proportion for the split municipalities is 0.185. If spatial segregation is higher among unified municipalities $(D_u > D_s)$, it means that they have a greater tendency to have proportional values that are divergent from the 0.300 mark than the tendency of split municipalities to have proportional values that depart substantially from 0.185. But this fact tells us nothing about the comparative effects on the two groups of a dynamic operating across both.

The interesting point of reference is the county proportion. How does each group of municipalities vary in relation to this common proportion and how do they differ in this respect from one another? The assumption is that both groups are subject to the same regional sorting dynamic, and the corresponding hypothesis is that this dynamic produces different outcomes depending on the group of municipalities that is examined. If this hypothesis is to be tested, it requires that split and unified municipalities be compared with reference to a common benchmark.

There is another method of dealing with the matter of comparability. This method permits the comparison of D values for groups of cities such as the ones considered here on dimensions for which their overall proportions are quite different and does so by using the following steps:

1. A common proportional value is imposed upon both spatial aggregates. This is done by substituting the common value $(P_c)$ in the formula for computing D in

place of an internally derived mean proportion for unified cities ($P_u$) or a similar proportion for split municipalities ($P_s$).

2. The resulting D values are adjusted to eliminate the residual difference between them that is an artifact of the imposition of the common proportion ($P_c$).

The use of $P_c$ in the computation of both D values eliminates the problem that arises when the proportions of spatial aggregates differ. The reason that the respective D values are comparable under this modification is that each becomes a measure of the divergence of unit proportions ($P_i$) from the grand aggregate proportion ($P_c$) rather than the internal proportions of the two groups of municipalities ($P_u$, $P_s$). This modification of D requires some further adjustment to eliminate distortions, caused by using an exogenous proportional value, before index values can be reported. Such an adjustment can be routinely made, however (see Appendix for comments and technical details). The D values reported hereafter have been made comparable by modification and adjustment as per this discussion.

## Comparing Split and Unified Municipalities Using the Adusted Index of Dissimilarity

The two groups of St. Louis County municipalities will be compared on five dimensions of differentiation: race, income, occupation, education, and family structure. Data from the 1980 Census of Population are used to measure differences between the groups along these dimensions (Bureau of the Census 1983a).

Racial differences are assessed by computing adjusted D values for each group of municipalities using the proportions of the municipal, group, and county populations that are black.

For income the measures used are the proportions of the relevant populations with incomes below 125% of the poverty level. This particular figure was chosen because it offers better variance than the proportion below the poverty level, and because it is published for both large and small places.

For occupation, the proportion of the various labor forces that are managers or professionals is used. This is an occupational grouping that retains its distinctive identity in a post-industrial economy, whereas the distinction between white-collar and blue-collar workers has become somewhat blurred.

For education the proportion of persons 25 years old and older with four years of college or more is used. Again, this measure has better variance than the proportion that are high school graduates.

Finally, as a measure of family structure, married-couple families with children under eighteen years as a proportion of the total number of households is used.

The results of this comparison are reported in Table 5.2. Remember that a higher value for D indicates greater spacial segregation.

**Table 5.2. D Values for Unitied and Split Municipalities Compared with D values for Large and Small Randomized Groups of Municipalities**

|  | Race | Income | Occu-pation | Educa-tion | Family Structure |
|---|---|---|---|---|---|
| Unified Municipalities | 0.420 | 0.161 | 0.270 | 0.337 | 0.052 |
| Split Municipalities | 0.024 | 0.075 | 0.170 | 0.259 | 0.155 |
| Large Group | 0.523 | 0.201 | 0.258 | 0.325 | 0.083 |
| Small Group | 0.667 | 0.305 | 0.176 | 0.257 | 0.110 |
| Unified-Split Differences | 0.396 | 0.086 | 0.100 | 0.078 | −0.103 |
| Large-Small Differences | −0.144 | −0.104 | 0.082 | 0.068 | −0.027 |

These results clearly support the hypothesis that the boundaries of unified municipalities sort more effectively than the boundaries of split municipalities. On four out of five dimensions, unified municipalities have substantially higher levels of spatial segregation. The difference is greatest with respect to segregation by race. Only in terms of family structure are split municipalities more spatially segregated than unified municipalities.

It is useful to recall at this point the nature of the adjusted index of dissimilarity and the implications of these results for theoretical claims made in chapter 2. It should be emphasized that D is structured in such a way as to be a measure of the average eccentricity of spatial units with regard to some mean value (indigenous or imposed). In this analysis, these mean values are the proportions of persons or households countywide that bear certain characteristics. In comparison to county wide means, on four out of five dimensions, unified municipalities are more eccentric than split municipalities.

## Exploring for Artifactuality

The group of unified municipalities is a great deal larger than the group of split municipalities—thirty-eight to eight, in fact. There is reason to suspect that this difference in size biases the results in Table 5.2 in favor of the boundary configuration hypothesis. Specifically, because the number of split municipalities is very small, the variance of their proportional values might be small also. It is more likely that extreme values will be found among the unified municipalities given their considerably greater number. Since the weighted sum (summation $T_i$ times the absolute value of $P_i$ minus P) is sensitive to extreme values, the disparity in sample size alone might account for the reported results. This argument is that similar results would be produced for any two groups of municipalities with similar comparative sizes. To determine the validity of this argument the forty-six municipalities were regrouped by a process of random selection. Municipalities were listed in alphabetical order, and every fifth city, be ginning with number five, was included in the smaller group. The result was two groups of thirty-seven and nine municipalities.

Adjusted D values were computed for both groups on all five dimensions. If the foregoing argument is correct, the D values should indicate that there is substantially more spatial segregation among large-group municipalities. Results are reported in Table 5.2. Rows five and six of the table present differences in D values. The differences in row five pertain to Unified and split municipalities. The differences in row six are for large and small random groups of municipalities. Positive signs indicate that the D value of the larger group of municipalities is larger than the D value of the smaller group. Negative signs indicate just the opposite. The numerical entries indicate the magnitude of the differences in D Values.

Comparing these two rows permits us to test the argument that the results of the analysis of segregation in unified and split municipalities are simply an artifact of sample size. If that were true, the signs of the differences reported in rows five and six should not vary across rows. These signs clearly do vary, however. On three of five dimensions, the polarity of the relationships is reversed. In other words, on the dimensions of race, income, and family structure, the smaller group of municipalities was more spatially segregated than the larger group, rather than less segregated. This table offers some evidence that methods used herein will not produce similar results for any combination of a large and a small group of municipalities.

## Intra-Municipal Segregation

These results would indicate that there is less segregation by race and socioeconomic status (at least in terms of evenness of distribution of these characteristics across spatial units) among split municipalities than among unified municipalities. Such a pattern of *inter*-municipal segregation, however, is compatible with any number of patterns of *intra*-municipal segregation. What should one expect of segregation within the split municipalities themselves? Either of two diametrically opposed expectations can be theoretically justified.

On one hand, it might be that suburban municipalities that are split by school district boundaries would exhibit high levels of segregation among neighborhoods. Such segregation would be structured by the school district boundary inasmuch as persons with certain racial and class characteristics would be attracted to one district, and persons with different characteristics would be attracted to the other. In other words, one might expect that variance in socioeconomic status and race would occur at the school district boundary, with one racially and socioeconomically identifiable group living in one district, and a socioeconomically and racially distinct group living in the other. A pattern such as this, produced by sorting at the school district boundary, should result in high levels of intra-municipal segregation by race and class.

Such a pattern would only be expected to emerge, however, if there were substantial differences in the school districts which served a particular municipality. For instance, suppose a municipality were split between two school districts, one of which had high expenditures per student and an excellent academic reputation, the other of which spent considerably less per student and was undistinguished academically. There should be broad differences in the municipal population corresponding to the boundary between the two districts. The district with greater expenditures and better academic programs would be more likely to attract middle class families which place high importance on education, and which are more likely to have the resources to acquire such favored locations. Lower income families should be more prevalant in the less academically distinctive district, presumably because they would be more able to afford housing there, and because they would be less likely in any case to pay the premium for higher quality educational programs on the assumption that they value education less. A pattern of settlement such as this would produce the type of results obtained from the analysis of cross-municipal segregation. The group of split municipalities would appear less segregated because the differential sorting across the school district boundary would result in municipal populations that were socially diverse.

If there are no such differences between the school districts that serve split municipalities, how can the fact that split municipalities appear to be less segregated than unified municipalities be explained? What would account for their greater social heterogeneity? Theoretically, such heterogeneity could result on the supposition that the crossing of school district and municipal boundaries produces ambiguous cues for persons engaged in housing search. For instance, if a settler were to ask a local acquaintance, "Now what school district would my kids be in if we bought that little place in Shrewsbury?", the answer would be "It might be Webster Groves, or it might be Affton." If the quality of schools is important to such a person, a final decision on the Shrewsbury location would require procuring information about both districts. At that point, the settler might simply filter the Shrewsbury location out of the search process, reasoning that alternatives in Kirkwood, Ballwin, and Manchester appear potentially just as satisfactory, and the task of learning about schools is simplified since each municipality is served by a single school district.

In sum, the pattern of lower spatial segregation across split municipalities could be produced by either of two opposing patterns of segregation within such municipalities—high segregation structured by school district boundaries, or relative lack of segregation. Which of these patterns characterizes split municipalities in St. Louis County?

*Exploratory Regression Analysis*

In order to determine the degree of internal segregation of split municipalities relative to unified municipalities, an index of dissimilarity value was computed for each of eighteen municipalities in St. Louis County. The number of municipalities was limited to eighteen because tract level data are not reported for the other twenty-eight municipalities included in the earlier analysis. Since their population is less than 10,000, data for these municipalities by census tract is not available. (The computation of a D value for any municipality requires that there be data for at least two spatial units within that municipality). Of these eighteen municipalities, five were split between two or more school districts, while thirteen were each basically served by one school district.

The resulting D values were regressed against the population size, the year of incorporation, and a dichotomous split-municipality variable for each municipality. Since eighteen cases is already painfully few for performing regression, the number of variables was limited to preserve degrees of freedom. Population size was entered as a control since larger municipalities might be expected to be more racially diverse and thus to have higher D values. The year of incorporation was also entered as a control. Previous studies have noted that increasing age among suburbs is associated with higher levels of segregation. Also, year of incorporation in St. Louis County is roughly commensurate with distance from the urban core, since near suburbs were incorporated predominantly during the late nineteenth and early twentieth centuries, and more peripheral suburbs were incorporated predominantly in the middle of the twentieth century. A control for distance from the urban core is useful since much evidence indicates that blacks are more likely to find residences in suburbs near to the central city.

These controls are relevant to any interpretation of the coefficient on the dichotomous split-municipality variable for which split municipalities are given a value of one, unified municipalities a value of zero. If split municipalities are more likely to be internally segregated across school district boundaries, their D values should be higher, producing a positive coefficient on the dichotomous variable. Such a result would be more credible in the presence of controls for municipal size, age, and distance from the urban core, since it will be attributable to some characteristic of the split municipalities other than these considerations. On the other hand, a negative coefficient would indicate that split municipalities are less likely to be internally segregated than unified municipalities, considerations of age, size, and distance being equal.

Estimated model coefficients are presented in Table 5.3 for dependent variables corresponding to each of four substantive dimensions of segregation: race, occupation, education, and family status. The dichotomous variable is not significant in any of these models, causing skepticism about any very literal translation of the coefficient into substantive conclusions. Furthermore, the coefficients are not large, and indicate that splitting municipalities has a small absolute effect on the magnitude of the index of dissimilarity. In the maximal case, if the coefficient is to be trusted, the D value for race is reduced about eight and a half points for split municipalities. For other dimensions, the reduction is in the neighborhood of one or two points. The signs on the dichotomous variable coefficient are negative for all four estimated models. If these results indicate anything, it is that split municipalities are *less segregated* internally than unified municipalities. This finding tends to support the second interpretation of the results of the analysis of cross-municipal segregation— that is, that split municipalities are less segregated as a group than unified municipalities because crossing municipal and school district boundaries provide ambiguous cues that do not support efficient sorting of persons by race and class.

## Examining Specific Cases

An examination of the five split municipalities included in the regression analysis validates the preceding conclusion. School districts providing services for each split municipality are compared on salient characteristics.

## Table 5.3. Regression of Index of Dissimilarity Values against Population, Year of Incorporation, and the Split Municipality Dummy

*OCCUPATION:*

|  | B | Std. E. | t | Beta |
|---|---|---|---|---|
| Constant | -0.70 | 0.95 | -0.73 | 0.00 |
| Population | 0.00 | 0.00 | 2.20 | 0.62 |
| Incorporation | 0.00 | 0.00 | 0.80 | 0.23 |
| Dummy | -0.01 | 0.03 | -0.52 | -0.12 |

$R^2$: 0.28

*EDUCATION:*

| | | | | |
|---|---|---|---|---|
| Constant | 0.59 | 1.19 | -0.49 | 0.00 |
| Population | 0.00 | 0.00 | 2.19 | 0.62 |
| Incorporation | 0.00 | 0.00 | 0.55 | 0.16 |
| Dummy | -0.02 | 0.04 | -0.52 | -0.12 |

$R^2$: 0.29

*RACE:*

| | | | | |
|---|---|---|---|---|
| Constant | 4.16 | 3.69 | 1.13 | 0.00 |
| Population | 0.00 | 0.00 | 0.08 | 0.03 |
| Incorporation | -0.00 | 0.00 | -1.04 | -0.34 |
| Dummy | -0.08 | 0.11 | -0.73 | -0.19 |

$R^2$: 0.12

*FAMILY STATUS:*

| | | | | |
|---|---|---|---|---|
| Constant | -0.80 | 1.18 | -0.68 | 0.00 |
| Population | 0.00 | 0.00 | 1.09 | 0.34 |
| Incorporation | 0.00 | 0.00 | 0.76 | 0.25 |
| Dummy | -0.02 | 0.04 | -0.60 | -0.16 |

$R^2$: 0.11

N = 18 for all models.

In terms of racial composition, expenditure per student, tax rate, and assessed valuation per student, there are not substantial differences among districts except for the case of Richmond Heights. Hence there is no reason to expect that different school districts would attract populations that are markedly different from each other in terms of social composition. With the exception of Richmond Heights, these split municipalities are less segregated in the aggregate than the unified municipalities because their municipal boundaries are less effective in sorting settlers by racial and socioeconomic characteristics.

There are substantial differences in the two school districts which serve the western half of Richmond Heights (Ladue and Clayton Districts) and the school district which serves the eastern half (Maplewood-Richmond Heights), however. Given these differences in expenditure, racial composition, taxation, and district wealth, one would expect that there would also be sizeable differences in the populations of western and eastern Richmond Heights. Values of D computed for Richmond Heights appear to validate this expectation. Of the eighteen cities for which individual D values are computed, Richmond Heights is the third most segregated by race, and has fairly high segregation values for education and occupation. For other split municipalities, because there are few differences among school districts, the boundary that divides them tends to be invisible. Because there are consequential differences in the school districts serving Richmond-Heights, school district boundaries within the city may be quite visible to persons making location decisions. This possibility will be investigated in greater detail in the following chapter.

## Conclusion

The terminology, numbers, and superscripts required by the preceding discussion do not encourage an intuitive grasp of the argument. This is an appropriate place to simplify and reiterate.

A fundamental perception of this study is that metropolitan areas are subject to a dynamic which has as its basic constituent the location decisions made by persons settling in these areas. In making these decisions, settlers obtain what information they can in order to exercise locational preferences. Political boundaries structure and, in a sense, carry information that is used by settlers. The configuration of boundaries has an impact on the way they structure information and the amount of information they carry. Boundaries that cross structure information less clearly than boundaries that coincide. Settlers receive weaker signals from crossing boundaries. Therefore, jurisdictions that are crossed by the boundaries of other jurisdictions should have less eccentric populations.

Split (or crossed) municipalities and unified municipalities in St. Louis County have been examined. An analysis of data for these municipalities indicates that split municipalities are, in fact, less eccentric than unified municipalities. Though this result is only suggestive, given the small number of cases examined, it is in conformity with the hypothesis about boundary configuration.

## Appendix

The comparability acquired by using "adjusted D" is purchased at the price of a further distortion of the D values that are thus produced.

This distortion can best be explained by beginning with a discussion of the alteration of the substantive interpretation of the D statistic that results from the imposition of the common proportion on both spatial aggregates. When the "indigenous" proportions of spatial aggregates are used to compute D, its interpretation is straightforward. Winship phrases it this way:

> The index of dissimilarity is equal to the ratio between the number of households that actually have to move and the maximum number that would have to move for any distribution of housing. . . . The index is equal to the proportion of households that still need to move in order to achieve complete desegregation (Winship 1977: 1061).

This interpretation is obviously incorrect once $P_c$ is substituted into equation 1. The reason is that no aggregate such as our group of split or of unified municipalities can achieve integration in terms of an exogenously imposed mean proportion that differs from its own.

For instance, suppose that the overall proportion of college graduates for the group of unified municipalities is 0.300, and that the county mean is 0.330. The best that can be done is for each municipality to achieve a proportion of 0.300 by using 0.330 in formula 1 and computing a D value for the unified municipalities. But no one can expect that the unified municipalities can ever be integrated in accordance with the 0.330 standard. There simply aren't enough college graduates to go around so that they number thirty-three percent of the population of each municipality. Having imposed a common proportion, then, it can no longer be claimed that D represents the proportion of the population that needs to move in order to achieve complete desegregation at $P_i = P = 0.330$ for all i. The value of D now represents the proportion of the population that would have to move in order to approximate *as nearly as possible* integration at the 0.330 level.

The important part of the formula for this discussion is again the numerator of the right hand term

$$(2) \quad \sum_{i=1}^{n} T_i |P_i - P|$$

When this term reaches its minimum value, spatial integration is maximized. The value of this term grows smaller as the values of the various $P_i$ approximate P. In the case where $P = P_c$, the externally imposed common proportion, the term reaches its minimum value when $P_i = P_g$ for all i (where $P_g$ is the internally derived group proportion). That is, when perfect spatial integration has been achieved in terms of the group proportion, the closest approximation possible to perfect integration defined in terms of the externally imposed proportion has also been reached. But when $P_c$ is substituted for P in equation 1, even though the spatial aggregate is as integrated as can be, the value of D is not zero. The above expression becomes

$$(3) \quad |P_g - P_c| \sum_{i=1}^{n} T_i$$

Since $P_g$ is not equal to $P_c$, this expression must have a positive value. Thus

$$(4) \quad D_c = \frac{|P_g - P_c| \sum_{i=1}^{n} T_i}{2TP(1-P)} > \emptyset$$

This, then, is the nature of the distortion of D that is produced when the externally derived common proportion $P_c$ is imposed upon different spatial aggregates that are to be compared. Even under perfect integration, D for each aggregate will have a residual positive value. To the extent that $P_g$ differs from $P_c$, therefore, D will be inflated.

Now for this application, $P_g$ will be replaced either by $P_u$, the overall proportion for the unified municipalities, or $P_s$, the overall proportion for the split municipalities. In turn, equation 1 will produce values for $D_u$, the measure of spatial segregation among unified municipalities, or $D_s$, the measure of spatial segregation among split municipalities. If a meaningful comparison of these values is to be made, one must know which has been most inflated by the substitution of $P_c$ and compensate for the difference between them.

The general form for determining the degree to which each D value has been inflated is given by equation 4. Thus if one wishes to know the extent of distortion entailed by calculating $D_u$ using the common proportion $P_c$, one must substitute appropriate values and solve

$$(5) \quad D_u{}^* = \frac{|P_u - P_c| \displaystyle\sum_{i=1}^{n} T_i}{2T_u P_c(1 - P_c)} = \frac{P_u - P_c}{2P_c(1 - P_c)}$$

where $D_u{}^*$ is equal to the residual value of $D_u$ under perfect integration among unified municipalities. The extent to which $D_s$ is distorted can be calculated using the same formula, substituting s for the subscript u.

If $D_{du}$ and $D_{ds}$ represent deflated values of $D_u$ and $D_s$, the following equations result:

$$(6) \quad D_{du} = D_u - D^*{}_u$$
$$(7) \quad D_{ds} = D_s - D^*{}_s$$

The values of $D_{du}$ and $D_{ds}$ can be meaningfully compared. When one is greater than the other, it is an indication of greater spatial segregation.

# 6

## A Case in Point:
## Richmond Heights, Missouri

Previous chapters have offered evidence that a sorting dynamic mediated by political boundaries is actually in place. This chapter presents anecdotal evidence that individuals *do* refer to political boundaries when making locational decisions. It also offers an example of a jurisdiction in which development has been strongly influenced by the presence of political boundaries.

In every community or school district, there are a number of individuals in a position to be aware of the locations of political boundaries and the spatial relationships among them. They also come into frequent contact with realtors and with persons making locational decisions.

Many of these people take it as a matter of course that persons moving into a metropolitan area seek out political boundaries and use them as references in deciding upon a location. For instance, when I first went to the offices of the Ladue School District to explore boundary configurations, the receptionist was unable to help me for several minutes while she carried on a telephone conversation with a prospective resident. This person asked detailed questions about the academic programs, facilities, accreditation, and personnel of the Ladue District. Afterward, the receptionist said that it was not unusual to receive such calls from persons moving into St. Louis County, and that providing information on the quality of Ladue schools was simply part of her routine duties.

The information supplied is apt to be quite impressive. Ladue has the second highest assessed valuation per pupil of St. Louis County school districts (only Clayton, Ladue's prestigious neighbor to the east, is higher). The Ladue District regularly wins awards for its academic excellence. It offers a diverse and interesting curriculum and an excellent faculty. More generally, the name "Ladue" carries a great deal of prestige in St. Louis County. The City of Ladue encompasses what is perhaps the county's most exclusive residential acreage (there might be some dispute on this account in favor of small sanctuaries of wealth such as Frontenac, Huntleigh Village, and Country Life Acres).

It is not surprising, therefore, that the city clerk of Frontenac, Missouri, the major portion of which is served by Ladue schools, claims that "a lot of real estate is sold [in Frontenac] because of the Ladue School District."

The Beau Jardin apartment complex is actually split by the Ladue School District boundary. One of the most interesting indications of the significance of political boundaries is that apartments that lie within the Ladue District carry higher rents than comparable apartments situated across the line.

Visits to city halls produced similar experiences. Shrewsbury, for instance, is a white, working class community of just over 5,000 in South St. Louis county. Shrewsbury is divided between the Webster Groves and Affton School Districts. The city administrator and receptionist were quite helpful in tracing the exact location of the boundary between the two districts within the city limits of Shrewsbury. I explained to them my interest in this project, and expressed my intuition that Shrewsbury residents probably saw little difference in living in the Webster Groves or the Affton District. "Oh no, people out here pay a lot of attention to whether they're in Webster Groves or Affton," the receptionist said at that point. "A lot of people don't want to pay Webster Groves taxes."

Webster Groves School District has a good academic reputation, and district residents have been consistently willing to support their schools financially. In the face of declining revenues due to population loss, the tax levy has repeatedly been increased. As of 1981, Webster Groves had the second highest tax rate of school districts in St. Louis County. Educational taxes in Webster Groves are $1.03 higher per one hundred dollars assessed valuation than in Affton.

If the perception of the people at Shrewsbury City Hall is correct, then there are complementary movements structured by the school district boundary. Persons whose chief concern is with tax levels will be drawn into Affton. Others, for whom education is a high priority, will be more likely to move into Webster Groves.

A visit to the St. Ann City Hall produced a similar experience. I told the receptionist that I was trying to locate the boundary between the Ritenour and Pattonville School Districts as it fell within the City of St. Ann. She commented that she supposed I was moving to St. Ann and wanted to make sure that I lived in Pattonville. I replied that I was not moving into St. Ann, but I was interested in people that did. The receptionist told me that the Pattonville school district had recently received national recognition, and that people moving into St. Ann for one reason or another frequently sought out residences within Pattonville's boundaries.

While at the Ladue School district offices, I spoke with Mrs. Rosemary Knobloch, a former administrative secretary of the Ladue District, who told me that she and her husband had wanted their children to attend Clayton Schools, but that they couldn't at the time (1952) afford housing within the City of Clayton. Consequently, they bought a home on the northern edge of the City of Richmond Heights, an area that fell just within the Clayton School District.

The point to be made here is that urban political boundaries do provide important cues to persons that are making locational decisions. These anecdotes demonstrate that people seek out boundary lines, often with considerable tenacity, as in the case of Mrs. Knobloch. Persons who have strong preferences regarding locations use urban political boundaries to gain information which enables them to realize their preferences.

The remainder of this chapter focuses on Richmond Heights, Missouri. Because of a happy coincidence of school district and census tract boundaries, Richmond Heights makes an interesting case study. A historical analysis of boundary relationships and an examination of population characteristics and economic development indicate that the placement of school district boundaries has been important in determining present conditions in Richmond Heights.

## Richmond Heights

There are several good reasons for choosing Richmond Heights for closer scrutiny. First, Richmond Heights is a prototype of urban fragmentation. A number of cities in St. Louis County are split between school districts, but Richmond Heights is the "most" split. Richmond Heights is divided between not just two or three different districts, but four—Clayton, Ladue, Brentwood, and Maplewood-Richmond Heights. Indeed, school district boundaries divide Richmond Heights into five discrete segments. Two separate areas of Richmond Heights, one in the east, one in the west, fall within Clayton School District boundaries.

The argument has been made that cross-cutting political boundaries transmit ambiguous messages to persons making locational decisions. When messages are transmitted, their content is likely to vary across school district boundaries. The result should be that fragmented municipalities have populations that are relatively heterogeneous as opposed to unified municipalities which should have eccentric and homogeneous populations. Richmond Heights should certainly be heterogeneous since it is particularly fragmented.

Furthermore, the fragmentation of Richmond heights goes beyond formal jurisdictional considerations. There are substantial differences between the school districts that serve Richmond Heights. In particular, Ladue and Clayton are the wealthiest, and possibly the most prestigious, school districts in the county. Because of this wealth, both districts are able to provide excellent programs while levying comparatively light taxes. Maplewood-Richmond Heights does not tax at a particularly high rate, but the result is that it spends considerably less on each pupil than Clayton or Ladue.

A second reason for considering Richmond Heights, in addition to its theoretical interest, is practicality. Happily, 1980 census tract boundaries very nearly approximate school district boundaries in Richmond Heights. The portion of Richmond Heights west of Hanley Road is divided between Ladue, Clayton, and Brentwood Districts. The southern fragment falling within Brentwood is of negligible importance, however, since it contains no residences. Ladue and Clayton remain. The differences between these districts are minimal. Both are prestigious, white, upper middle class school districts. Fortunately, census tract 2166 is coterminous with this half of the city.

The majority of Richmond Heights east of Hanley Road is served by the Maplewood-Richmond Heights District. The northeastern corner of the city is within the Clayton School District, but most of this area is commercial. A substantial area is occupied by St. Mary's Hospital and a smaller, opthalmic hospital. It is doubly fortunate that census tracts 2167 and 2168 together are exactly coterminous with this eastern half of Richmond Heights.

Hanley Road, then, divides Richmond Heights into two rather different pieces in terms of the public education that is available in each. Richmond Heights west of Hanley Road falls within school districts that offer every educational advantage. East of Hanley Road, Richmond Heights lies principally within the boundaries of a much less well-endowed school district, one with less money to spend and without the prestige of its neighbors. The interesting question is whether there are broad differences in the characteristics of persons living to the east and west of Hanley Road in Richmond Heights. The advantage that Richmond Heights offers, because census tract boundaries follow the boundaries of these two parts of the city, is that the presence and extent of such differences can be determined with fair precision. The population of the eastern and western parts are also the populations of census tract 2166 and census tracts 2167 and 2168 respectively, and detailed data are available for census tract populations.

## A Chicken-and-Egg Story

Even if it is found that there are substantial differences between the populations of the two halves of Richmond Heights, an ambiguity remains. Have these populations structured school district boundaries? Have school district boundaries been drawn to conform to existing patterns of residential settlement, as a manifestation of the residents' shared consciousness that they constitute a community? Or have such patterns arisen in response to school district boundaries already in place? If it should be found that eccentric populations have manipulated school district boundaries in order to reinforce some common racial, cultural, or socioeconomic identity, then a sense of community must have preceded the existence of the boundary. Such a finding does not prove that urban political boundaries do not support recruitment, but it is an indication that they are less interesting in this respect than one might have wished. On the other hand, if it should be the case that the school district boundaries in question have remained unchanged for a very long period of time, the case is strengthened. There are grounds for arguing that the boundaries have shaped an eccentric population by transmitting cues to persons marking locational decisions.

In the case of Richmond Heights, school district boundaries have been stable for a remarkably long time.

## School District History in St. Louis County

School district organization has an interesting history in St. Louis County. The structure of school districts in the county in the late Nineteenth Century can be recovered using tax records (Detering 1955). These records indicate that the forerunners of the present districts were frequently in existence as early as 1877. Such districts were identified by a sequence of three numbers—a district number, township number, and a range number. A school district in St. Louis County might typically have been identified as District 1, Township 45, Range 6. Indeed, when the state mandated this scheme in 1874, its approach to bounding a school district was essentially geometric. A grid was imposed on the county map which created geographical units of regular size and shape. The units that were already populated become active school districts. As development continued and additional units were populated, they were also constituted school districts and were added to the tax roles.

Significantly, there is no evidence that this system gave much consideration to bases for drawing school district lines other than geometry (Detering 1955: 28). In particular, this procedure appears to have been relatively oblivious to any natural topographic boundaries, and of community lines constituted prior to the imposition of the boundary grid. The boundaries that were created in this fashion followed the logic of administrative convenience.

Great portions of St. Louis County were unpopulated at this time, though further development was anticipated. The grid system must have seemed an efficient, fair way of organizing the provision of an essential public service during a period of rapid population growth and economic development. It accomodated existing service delivery requirements and was sufficiently flexible to meet future needs. There was a capacity to expand educational government almost modularly to keep pace with an expanding population. This capacity would have been seriously impaired had the process of geographic definition of districts been made to await a fortuitous combination of topo

graphic features and the emergence of community identity. In other words, the population might have expanded
into an area that was not topographically distinct. A substantial number of children might have been denied educational services for a considerable time—the period of
time required for the expanding population to occupy a topographically defined geography, to see the lack of educational services as a problem, and to acquire consciousness
of themselves as a community which, further, should orga-
nize to supply services publicly. The grid system eased the
process of the geographic definition of new educational
districts by supplying predefined spatial units, and it supported a preexisting administrative mechanism for constituting school districts in a way responsive to objective
need.

It is important to emphasize, however, that the grid
system of school district definition was designed to function according to the needs of state and county authorities
to administer the provision of educational services in a
growing area: it was not meant to be responsive to the de-
sires of local populations. It did not very easily take into
account considerations of community identity. Such communities might, or might not, conform to boundary configurations imposed by the grid. The grid system implied a
geometric, regular division of geography into political
units. But commonalities of race, religion, nationality, or
socioeconomic status might well follow geographic patterns different than those built into the grid. Particularly
with the passage of time, as demographic flux was replaced by increasingly stable residential patterns, one can
imagine that local communities chafed under a system
which was insensitive to their concerns and identities.

This procedure for designating school districts was
abandoned in 1910. At this time, the County Court of St.
Louis County renamed all of the county's school districts
(County Court of St. Louis County 1910). The nature
of this renaming is more interesting than its actual sub-
stance. District names corresponding to grid positions
were eliminated. The court assigned names to the dis-

tricts that in many cases corresponded to topographic features—Pea Ridge, Cold Water (Creek), Columbia Bottom—or communities—Black Jack, Scudder, Kinlock.

This reconstituting of names may also well have represented a change in the philosophy of school district definition in the county. The geometric approach, predicted upon the flexible and efficient administration of education services in the context of growth and development, appears to have been supplanted by a community approach which emphasized the provision of education services to communities that were already in existence. Whereas the former approach yields a system that is readily expandable to permit extension of services under fluid circumstances with minimum delay, the latter suffers delay willingly in the interest of tailoring the delivery of educational services to the requirements and preferences of existing communities. The shift from one approach to the other probably reflects a gradual change in the county from one of a few young, unselfconscious communities to one of an increased number of communities with more clearly defined socioeconomic identities. There is some support for this interpretation in the fact that many of the older, originally independent municipalities of St. Louis County were incorporated around this time—Brentwood (1919), Clayton (1913), Glendale (1912), Maplewood (1908), Richmond Heights (1913), Shrewsbury (1913), University City (1906), Valley Park (1917), Webster Groves (1896).

The change in school district organization ordered by the County Court may well represent a point which must come in the development of any area—a point at which the people who settle that area cease to be merely an aggregate and come to think of themselves as a community with a particular character, purpose, and interest. This character, purpose, and interest, are likely to arise out of objective bases of commonality—social class, ethnicity, religion, language. In turn, the preservation of character, purpose, identity, and interest, in the minds of those who comprise the community, may well hinge upon the exclusion of those who do not share these objective bonds. A change in sorting dynamics is likely to take place at this point, from one in which boundaries structure populations to one in which self-conscious populations manipulate boundaries. At this point also, exclusion is likely to arise as a complement to recruitment.

After this renaming of school districts, the grid system disappeared in outlying areas of St. Louis County. Particularly during the late 1940s and early 1950s, in the presence of the threat of mandatory merger under the School District Reorganization Law of 1947 (Senate Bill 307), the very large school districts on the county's northern and western peripheries (Rockwood, Parkway, Hazelwood) were created from the numerous small districts that had existed under the grid system. There was very little change, however, in many of the districts contiguous with the western boundary of the City of St. Louis. This area was developed and was considerably less fluid economically and demographically than more remote areas. Vestiges of the grid system of school district demarcation, which was in place prior to the stabilization of population and economic development, persist in the near-west county to the present time.

The present concern is with the histories of the Ladue, Maplewood-Richmond Heights, and Clayton Districts. All of these districts lie in the near-western corridor of St. Louis County, clustered around Highway Forty, just west of the city of St. Louis. The boundaries of two of these three school districts have remained extremely stable.

The Clayton School District first appears on county tax ledgers as District 10, Township 45, Range 6 in 1880 (Detering 1955). It became a village school district in 1906, but its boundaries did not change. District 10 was renamed the Clayton School District by the County Court in 1910, but again, the boundaries remained unaltered. The records of the St. Louis County Board of Education and the Clayton Board of Education indicate that Clayton School District boundaries have been altered only once in 104 years. In 1952, nine lots near the intersection of Buck and Everett Avenues were transferred by special election from Brentwood School District to Clayton. This was a relatively minor change, probably motivated by the fact that the path of Highway Forty separates these lots from the rest of Brentwood District. Both districts probably agreed that all parties would be better served were the nine lots to be transferred to Clayton.

Maplewood-Richmond Heights first appears on tax ledgers as District 3, Township 45, Range 6 in 1877. It wasorganized as a village school district in 1906 and was renamed the Maplewood City School District by the County Court in 1910. In 1937, Maplewood became Maplewood-Richmond Heights. In spite of these changes in name and organization, however, no evidence can be found that the boundaries of what is today the Maplewood-Richmond Heights School District have changed in any way in 107 years (Detering 1955).

There have been considerable changes in the boundaries of the Ladue School District. Ladue has been formed from four school districts that appeared on county tax ledgers in 1877 as District 8, Township 45, Range 6; District 6, Township 45, Range 5; District 1, Township 45, Range 6; and District 2, Township 45, Range 5 (Detering 1955). In 1910, the County Court designated these districts the Price, Wright, Central, and Spoede School Districts respectively. In 1936, Price and a part of Rock Hill District became the Ladue Town School District. In 1942, Central, which had become known as Olivette, was annexed to Ladue; and Wright and Spoede were annexed in 1949 and 1951 respectively (Detering 1955; St. Louis County Department of Education 1955). In 1951, a parcel of land was transferred from Ritenour School district to Ladue (St. Louis County Council 1951).

In spite of these numerous changes, the eastern portion of Ladue which is of principal concern has not changed. The western-most part of Richmond Heights has for its entire history fallen within the boundaries of the original nucleus of Ladue—the old Price School District, or what in 1877 was District 8, Township 45, Range 6. Ladue's expansion has taken place to the south, west, and north, leaving the geographical relationship between the City of Richmond Heights and what has become the Ladue School District unchanged for 107 years.

The point to be made here is that if differential development is found that corresponds to school district boundaries, it cannot be assumed that the City of Richmond Heights developed in this fashion and then school district boundaries were changed to coincide with distinct areas. The boundaries of the districts in question as they lay within Richmond Heights have not changed significantly since 1880. Indeed, these boundaries predate the incorporation of the city, which occurred in 1913 (St. Louis County Department of Planning 1982).

### Differential Development

There has been differential development in Richmond Heights east and west of Hanley Road.

There is considerable commercial development throughout Richmond Heights along such major thoroughfares as Brentwood Boulevard, Clayton Road, and Big Bend Boulevard. Much of this development consists of storefront businesses—bicycle sales and repair, real estate, baked goods, florists, short order restaurants, service stations, super markets, food specialty shops.

There are two notable exceptions to this pattern. First, in the western portion of Richmond Heights, lying within the Ladue District, there is no commercial development. This is exclusively an area of single family houses, much of it on large lots. Second, larger enterprises are found somehow in those portions of Richmond Heights that lie within the Clayton School District. The West Roads/Galleria Shopping Center, for instance, is within the Clayton District in Richmond Heights west of Hanley Road. It includes a large department store and shops and boutiques that cater to the designer market. Across Brentwood Boulevard is a modern high-rise office complex

occupied mostly by clinics and offices of medical special-
ists. Two hospitals are located in the eastern portion
where the boundaries of Clayton District once again dip
into Richmond Heights. St. Mary's is a large, comprehensive medical facility. Across Bellevue Avenue from St.
Mary's is a smaller eye hospital which has recently petitioned to become a full-service hospital.

Commercial development in Richmond Heights, then,
tends to be comprised of small, family owned businesses
that employ relatively few people in low-level white collar,
blue collar, and service positions. But areas of Richmond
Heights outside of Maplewood-Richmond Heights School
District provide the exceptions to this rule. In the Ladue
School District there is no commercial development at all.
In the two separate pieces of the Clayton District, there
are also numerous small businesses. But there are several
sizable concerns that employ large numbers of people in
professional and administrative positions.

There is considerable variety in residential development in Richmond Heights. Housing west of Hanley Road
consists almost entirely of single family dwellings. East of
Hanley Road are significant numbers of multi-unit dwellings—duplexes and apartment buildings.

Residential areas west of Hanley Road include some
fairly exclusive real estate. Immediately west of Hanley
road is Lake Forest, an area of large homes. The theme of
the Lake Forest area is evidently "mountains of the west
coast." It is served by Rainier, Shasta, Sierra, Antler, and
Overcrest Drives. West of Lake Forest, in a triangle described by St. Louis Belt and Terminal railroad tracks,
U.S. Highway 40, and the Inner Belt Highway, is a small
area of more modest homes.

Moving west, the landscape is dominated by commercial development until one passes Brentwood Boulevard
and approaches Ladue. Then, residential areas reap-
pear—Berkshire, Ridgetop, Mcknight Hills, Mcknight
Acres, Mcknight Orchard, Scarsdale, Laymont and Layton. These areas are crossed by streets such as Saranac
Drive, Green Ridge Drive, Stonebridge Drive, Thorndell

Drive, Ridgemont Drive, and Ashmere Drive. Houses in this area are large, stately and expensive.

East of Hanley Road on Ethel Avenue and Jones Avenue is found moderate and low income housing. On Wise Avenue north of Highway Forty are small brick and frame houses and duplexes. On Bellevue south of St. Mary's Hospital are two-flats, four-flats, and walkup apartment buildings. At the corner of Bellevue and Wise is an unkempt laundromat and a ramshackle convenience store serving the residents—predominantly renters—of the neighborhood sandwiched between the hospital and Clayton Road to the north and the expressway to the south. The corner is apt to have three of four bicycles laying around. It is a gathering place where young people in the neighborhood smoke, drink sodas, and participate in various adolescent rites of passage. Not infrequently of late, the participants include black children. (Blacks are not commonly seen on Ashmere or Shasta Drives except for the gardeners and maids that walk off buses and into the area in the morning, and then depart by bus at night.)

The notable exception to this pattern of housing is the area immediately east of Hanley Road and south of Clayton Road. Known as Hampton Park, this area is impressive by any standards. There is some tension between the social prestige of the Maplewood-Richmond Heights School District within which Hampton Park lies. This is a situation that has proven vexing to Hampton Park residents. Some of them resolve this tension by sending their children to private schools. Some children from Hampton Park attend Clayton schools as tuition—paying students (tuition is about $2600 a year). Hamptonians attempted a blanket solution recently by placing a proposition on the ballot that would have made Hampton Park part of the wealthier Clayton School District. The justification they offered for the proposed boundary change was that it would permit their children to attend school with their social peers. This was not justification enough for the voters of Maplewood-Richmond Heights School District who heavily defeated the proposition.

The differences in residential development are reflected in the fact that the median value of housing in Census Tract 2166 (West of Hanley Road) is $75,900, while the corresponding figures for tracts 2167 and 2168 (east of Hanley Road) are $39,500 and $37,100, respectively. Median contract rent in Richmond Heights west of Hanley Road is $198. For the two tracts east of Hanley Road it is $176 (2167) and $182 (2168).

## Socioeconomic and Demographic Differentials

Not only are there developmental differences between the areas east and west of Hanley Road, but there are consistent socioeconomic and demographic differences between the populations of these areas.

A higher proportion of households west of Hanley Road are comprised of married couple families with children under eighteen, though the differences are slight. There is also a small difference in median age, the median age of the population west of Hanley Road being about three years greater than the median age of the population in eastern Richmond Heights.

Residents of western Richmond Heights are better educated, on average, than their neighbors to the east. The proportion of high school graduates in tract 2166 is 0.890. It is 0.715 and 0.768 in tracts 2167 and 2168 respectively. In tract 2166 the proportion of college graduates is 0.424. It is 0.288 in tract 2167 and 0.277 in tract 2168.

The population west of Hanley Road contains a larger number of persons with prestigious occupations. Forty-four and seven-tenths percent are managers and professionals. About thirty-one percent of persons living in Richmond Heights east of Hanley road are managers and professionals.

Not surprisingly, since the westerners are slightly older, better educated, and have better jobs, they also make more money. The mean income of persons employed in the labor force in tract 2166 is $39,319. For such persons in tract 2167, the figure is $22,541. For persons employed in the labor force in tract 2168 the mean income is $17,112. The mean income for a married couple family with children under eighteen west of Hanley Road is $82,438. East of Hanley Road, in tract 2167, the mean family income is $35,533. In tract 2168, the mean family income is $24,575.

Finally, there has been considerable penetration of Richmond Heights east of Hanley Road by blacks. The population of eastern Richmond Heights is about nineteen percent black. The overwhelming majority of blacks in Richmond Heights, however, are concentrated in Census Tract 2167 which is thirty-four percent black. Census tract 2166 (west) is less than two percent black.

In sum, the typical resident of western Richmond Heights is white, affluent, and educated. He/she is relatively likely to have a high-prestige job. He/she is slightly more likely than persons living farther east in Richmond Heights to have children. These are precisely the sort of people that one would expect to be attracted to school districts like Clayton and Ladue. If the literature is correct, these are the people—middle class professionals—who most value education and who are most willing to pay the price for locations that provide access to good educational programs.

## Implications

Richmond Heights is an actual example of the "black-and-white" model of jurisdictional integration and heterogeneity presented in chapter 2 and discussed further in chapter 5. If half the area of a circle is colored black and half is colored white, then on average the circle is gray. This average result is very different from having a gray circle. Though on average the circles are the same, it is a fact that in the black and white circle no actual gray area can be said to exist.

Richmond Heights is presented as an example of a jurisdiction characterized by cross-cutting boundaries. It is perhaps the best example of such a jurisdiction in St. Louis County, and certainly the best example for which there are data.

Richmond Heights is, in fact, a heterogeneous city. Of all the municipalities in St. Louis County for which the Bureau of the Census publishes data, Richmond Heights most nearly approximates the county proportion black (approximately 14% for Richmond Heights as compared to 11% for St. Louis County). The percentage of poverty families in Richmond Heights is reasonably close to the county percentage (11% in Richmond Heights are below 125% of the poverty level as opposed to 7% in the County). Thirty-four percent of the work force in Richmond Heights are managers and professionals, while 28% of the county work force is among this occupational group. And about nine percent more of Richmond Heights' population are college graduates than the population of the entire county. It is neither black nor white, nor can it be characterized as rich or poor. Richmond Heights tends to attract low income and high income persons, blacks and whites, professionals and lower status workers, families and single persons, old and young people, in about the same proportions as they are present in the county as a whole.

This heterogeneity can be understood by recalling that Richmond Heights is divided by school district boundaries, and that these boundaries structure significant demographic and socioeconomic differences among the residents of the city. The proportion black in eastern Richmond Heights is higher than the county proportion black, while the proportion black in western Richmond Heights is much lower, and so on. Neither of these areas is heterogeneous, but averaging across areas produces the heterogeneity that characterizes Richmond Heights as a whole.

In other words, Richmond Heights is heterogeneous because school districts within Richmond Heights attract different types of people. The school districts themselves are distinctive. In western Richmond Heights, Clayton and Ladue provide very high quality educational programs. Maplewood-Richmond Heights in the east cannot spend nearly as much per pupil and does not enjoy the reputation of its western neighbors. The boundaries of these school districts provide settlers with the cues that they need to realize their locational preferences. Analyses have been presented in the previous chapter to support the argument that jurisdictions that are sub-divided by the boundaries of other jurisdictions should be less eccentric than jurisdictions that are not. Richmond Heights, once differing areas are averaged, represents a case which conforms to this analysis.

The development of Richmond Heights also offers an example of jurisdictions in which eccentricity has resulted because of the presence of political boundaries. Chapter 3 discussed the difficulty of determining the circumstances under which jurisdictions and, in turn, boundaries, were created. It is impossible in most cases to find out if jurisdictions were created by eccentric populations in recognition of a characteristic that members have in common, or if they were created in the absence of eccentricity simply to facilitate the delivery of some service. Hence, it is very difficult to assess the degree to which political boundaries play a casual role in the emergence of population eccentricity within jurisdictions.

Richmond Heights presents a strong case for concluding that boundaries can be causal in the creation of eccentric populations. The differences in the population of eastern and western Richmond Heights correspond to the location of school district boundaries within the city. These boundaries have been fixed since 1880. They were imposed by the state of Missouri in order to have some consistent system for organizing public education. They were not created by local authorities in recognition of already existing community lines. At this time, St. Louis County was sparsely populated. Very few of the municipalities that were eventually incorporated in the county had been incorporated by 1874, when the state legislature adopted this method of school district definition. (There were, in fact, only four—Bridgeton, Fenton, Florissant, and Kirkwood.) Indeed, in 1876 the City of St. Louis separated itself from St. Louis County, partially because tax bills were inflated by the expense of delivering services to the residents of thinly populated areas. A further indication of the degree to which these school district boundary lines ignored local communities was the fact that they were largely determined by a grid imposed upon St. Louis County by the state. The boundaries of school districts existing at this time reflected geometry more than community consciousness.

In short, it is difficult to believe that the correspondence between school district lines in Richmond Heights and broad, consistent differences in the population of the municipality exists because the school district boundaries have been manipulated to conform to population eccentricities. In point of fact, the school district boundaries have not been manipulated in over 100 years since they were first created. It is much more plausible that the differential development of eastern and western Richmond Heights is to some degree explained by the different characteristics of the Clayton and Ladue School Districts, on one hand, and the Maplewood-Richmond Heights School District on the other. The two more prestigious districts have attracted middle class, well-educated, professional residents; and the large commercial activities that are located within these districts have probably been attracted in part by the proximity of concentrations of affluent potential clients. The less prestigious district has attracted residents that do not have the resources to take advantage of the housing and educational opportunities offered by western Richmond Heights.

# 7

## Conclusions and Implications

In this final chapter, two points need to be clarified. The first has to do with the complementary relationship between the politics of exclusion and jurisdictional recruitment. The emphasis in this book has been to establish the necessity of recruitment; but it should be remembered that they are complementary components, not alternative explanations, of population sorting.

Also, clarification of the nature of housing markets and their role in urban population sorting is needed. Some would argue that market forces, like the laws of thermodynamics, are unavoidable, and that patterns of urban segregation should be understood as simply market outcomes. This study argues, however, that such outcomes are better explained by invoking politics, not economics.

It should be emphasized that the politics of boundary creation are uniquely American. Urban development and local government formation in other Western industrialized democracies are integrated into national policy in an attempt to serve collective interests. Local government formation in the United States, by contrast, is usually undertaken in the pursuit of parochial interests. Indeed, local government creation in the United States might be termed an act of "anti-government" insofar as its intent is to protect parochial interests from interference by overarching units of government representing the interests of a

165

more heterogeneous sample of the public. The result of anti-government is to produce "theme-park" suburbs on the one hand, and slums and ghettoes on the other. The politics of boundary creation in the United States permits some to enjoy pleasant life styles, security, and good services, while the costs of urbanization are concentrated and imposed on others.

This book has attempted to demonstrate that urban political boundaries are an important part of this urban development process. This argument has not been explicitly made elsewhere in the literature of urban studies. Other explanations of urban outcomes emphasize exclusionary powers that are exercised by metropolitan governments. There is no point to denying that these exclusionary powers exist and that they are responsible for a great deal of the sorting of populations that occurs in American cities. It is also clear, however, that exclusion alone cannot account for enduring segregation by race and class.

I have argued that the structure of urban political boundaries is no less important than the governments that it defines. Political boundaries support the recruitment that is the complement to exclusion in urban sorting. They are significant in themselves as a system of information, a frame of reference which provides cues to persons making locational decisions. Political boundaries are manifestations of the widespread recognition of **place,** a spatial unit with its own identity, separate and recognizable from other spatial units. Once discrete spatial units exist they can begin to acquire attributes, and it is possible to support sorting across urban geographies. Individual preferences are matched with the attributes of places in the calculus of persons making location decisions. Empirical evidence has been presented in chapters 4, 5, and 6 to indicate that such an information-based sorting dynamic is present in American urban centers.

In simple terms, the point of this book is that by creating numerous places, numerous cells within which urban populations can be segregated are also created.

## The Complementary Working of Exclusion
## and Recruitment

From chapter 1 on, exclusion and recruitment have been treated as if they were separate dynamics. The purpose of this book has been to demonstrate that there is a recruitment dynamic at work, and that it has important implications for the segregation of populations by certain salient characteristics, such as race and socioeconomic status. It has therefore been necessary to take a somewhat "polemical" tack with regard to exclusionary factors, counterposing them to recruitment factors, questioning their importance wherever possible, and emphasizing the effects of, as Schelling terms it, "aggregation rather than segregation".

It is not intended here that recruitment factors should be minimized when their importance has been repeatedly stressed through six chapters of work. But it should be recognized, though they are analytically separable, that recruitment and exclusion are actually components of a single dynamic. The socioeconomic and racial character of communities is a function both of the people that are attracted to them, and the people who, for whatever reason, end up living somewhere else. One can only meaningfully speak of the type of people that live in a certain area because at the same time implicit reference is made to all of those people who **do not** live there.

The segregation of American metropolitan areas, then, results from the complementary action of these two sub-dynamics. It is particularly important to realize that when it is determined that a metropolitan jurisdiction has become segregated due to exclusionary practices, one cannot conclude that the phenomenon has been completely explained or understood. The segregation in that jurisdiction cannot be ascribed simply to exclusion and left at that. For even where it is obvious that exclusion has been an important factor in creating segregation, it is still necessarily true that for segregation to be stably maintained, recruitment must also take place. As Anthony Downs indicates, "neighborhood stability never means lack of movement, especially of population." There is constant turnover in populations at a greater or lesser rate. "If a neighborhood is to be remain stable, these movers must be replaced by newcomers with similar characteristics" (Downs 1981: 24).

Indeed, this book argues that the relationship between exclusion and recruitment is so subtle that the transition from one to the other can be all but imperceivable. Each becomes the other with such facility that in some cases they genuinely cannot be separated. Hence, the occurrence of exclusion in most cases means the *de facto* occurrence or augmentation of recruitment. This is true to the extent that exclusion produces jurisdictional populations that are more easily identifiable by their socioeconomic characteristics. Increasing the identifiability of jurisdictions and jurisdictional populations augments the sense of place and necessarily sharpens sorting based upon recruitment. Where exclusionary sorting is successful, recruitment must also become more successful.

Such a complementary functioning of exclusion and recruitment is easy to imagine. There is considerable evidence to indicate that black settlers base their locational decision on the perception that some areas are open to black in-migration and others are not (for instance, Molotch 1972: 170–172; Logan and Schneider 1984: 886–887; Berry et al. 1976). This perception by blacks implies a two-step dynamic of racial segregation. The first step requires whites to engage in exclusionary activities which indicate to blacks that they are not welcome. These activities may or may not include overt hostility and violence toward blacks attempting to enter the area (Hirsch 1983). Repeated exclusionary actions against blacks are necessary in order to create the perception that a community is closed to them. The second step occurs when this perception is formed on the part of black settlers. At this point, their behavior is not a response to actual exclusionary encounters, but to information structured by the boundary of the community in question; information to the effect that their settlement in the community will be opposed by various means. The first step is exclusionary. The second step is a manifestation of recruitment—or, in the interest of semantical accuracy, one might better say dis-recruitment. This is an interesting example of the interactive nature of the relationship between exclusion and recruitment because, if it is apt, it indicates that recruitment can actually be substituted for exclusion. Jurisdictions that wish to remain segregated need not continually engage in costly and potentially dangerous exclusionary activity. They need only create the impression that such activity is likely, and then allow the disrecruitment mechanism to work.

There is no reason to assume that the relationship between exclusion and recruitment is always ordered in this way, however. It is probably frequently true that successful recruitment engenders efforts at exclusion. Where there are formal boundaries to define discrete spatial units and structure the choices of settlers, eccentric populations can be produced over time (see chapters 2 and 3). Once eccentricity reaches a certain point, it can suggest to residents the possibility and desirability of implementing exclusionary strategies. In effect, political boundaries in this process create latent groups. When the weight of commonality becomes great enough, these groups become conscious, define their interests, and use exclusionary power to pursue these interests. It is entirely plausible that young suburban jurisdictions on urban peripheries acquire their initial socioeconomic characters by recruitment. They attract young, middle class, white families, for instance, on the basis of their association with ordered and comfortable lifestyles, and their reputation for good schools. These white families use their relatively numerous resources to acquire locations in such jurisdictions. At this stage, recruitment may be all that is required for the community to maintain its character. As urban development proceeds, however (see Downs 1981: pp. 37–60 for one discussion of development) the life style of the community may be threatened by intruder groups. At this point, it requires little of one's imagination to think that residents develop an explicit awareness of their shared interest in preserving the community for persons similar to themselves, and that they take concerted action to exclude intruders.

It is reasonable to assume, therefore, that wherever there is significant segregation of populations by salient characteristics, there is probably a sorting dynamic at work based upon the complementary sub-dynamics of exclusion and recruitment.

The further significance of this statement lies in the fact that there is a substantial amount of segregation of populations across jurisdictional boundaries. And, if the examples of Cook County and Los Angeles County mean anything, segregation of this sort is extensive and increasing. In these cases, the boundaries themselves structure segregation by performing both exclusionary and recruitmental functions. The question is, if this is taken to be established, what does it imply for politics?

## The Nature of Markets

Devotees of the free market are prone to assume that market mechanisms and market outcomes are ethically and politically neutral. They frequently are puzzled by the commitment of considerable intellectual and social resources to the understanding and amelioration of urban segregation of various types. They tend to understand these patterns of segregation (or, in terms more congenial to their perspective, aggregation) as straightforward outcomes of persons acting upon individual preferences through the agency of markets. Their puzzlement has two sources. The first is that markets to them are analytical, not ethical, constructs. They consequently do not understand the righteous indignation with which some observers regard market outcomes. The second is that, even if the undesirability of certain market outcomes were to be granted on ethereal ethical grounds, they are nevertheless produced by the ineluctable workings of the market and therefore are not susceptible of change. These two points can be summarized by saying that some economically-minded observers of metropolitan affairs regard market outcomes as either ethically neutral, or akin to gravity in their physical necessity, or both. They therefore dismiss much of the work done on metropolitan spatial segregation as having no implication beyond simple description of circumstances.

Economicists are likely to assume the "givenness" of existing sets of market outcomes because they frequently do not consider markets in the context of the other types of systems with which they interact. They consider markets in isolation from other social phenomena and they use assumptions and methodologies that are self-consciously economic. This approach to markets requires that other understandings of social interactions and outcomes—in terms of social stratification, for instance—be either ignored or put through a process of conversion and baptism. The conversion is complete when concepts like status and social distance are assigned values and incorporated into the market process.

Such persons, preoccupied with narrowly conceived economic processes, might well react to the analysis of population sorting by saying "What you're really talking about here are simple market outcomes." This statement incorporates both the tendency to isolate markets from other social systems (and thereby to ignore such systems) and the tendency to give factors exogenous to markets market status. The purpose of the statement is to say in effect that no action is necessary. Economics has comprehended this state of affairs and it is exactly as economics says it should be.

To clarify matters it should be noted first of all that to say that population sorting is a market process does not prevent it from being information based or structured by political boundaries. Markets are themselves information systems and their functioning is frequently integrated with urban political boundary systems (Tiebout,

1956; Ostrom, Tiebout, and Warren, 1970). Prices comprise the information that animates markets, and one of the types of information that political boundaries convey is a fair indication of the price range of locations within various jurisdictions. In St. Louis County, for instance, the names of municipalities such as Clayton, Ladue, Valley Park, and Maplewood convey substantial market information about the price of housing. Boundaries define with greater precision the nature of the commodity that is offered in housing markets—a residential location with manifold lifestyle associations.

It should also be pointed out that markets are not static. The circumstances which determine market outcomes at a given time are subject to change. Markets do not exist in a vacuum, but are structured by their environments. Specifically, market outcomes at a particular time are often structured by recruitment outcomes at some previous time.

Molotch shows an awareness of the interdependence of market values and recruitment in his final chapter (Molotch 1972). He speaks of the ways in which places compete for people and resources (see also Lyons and Lowery 1986; Peterson 1981). In this competition, places use resources to attract additional resources. Additional resources are brought into places by people who own or command them. Hence, it can be said without too much distortion that places compete for the types of people who are likely to have resources.

Places, or, more accurately, people located in specific places, engage in this competition because they have an investment in their locations. If they attract people with resources, their investment remains secure. Indeed, the agglomeration of resources in a particular place increases the value of the resourses that were originally there.

Success in the competition between places for people, however, has implications for the complementary competition between people for places. Success comes when the value of land in a given place increases. But increasing the value of the land also increases the resources required to obtain a location within the place in question.

The competition of places for people is transparently a recruitment process. Places which offer a constellation of resources (one might even say a life style) congenial to the sorts of people who have resources to bring with them are effective in recruiting those people. In turn, the more attractive the place, the higher the bid required to obtain it, and hence, the greater the price of locations in that place. This result is just as transparently a market outcome.

It is not the case, then, that there are two discrete sets of outcomes, one set called "market outcomes", and another unrelated set called "boundary recruitment outcomes". The two are intrinsically related. If they are not synonymous, they are at least not separable, and market outcomes cannot be understood in isolation from recruitment. Therefore, to the extent that population sorting is based on recruitment, in cannot be dismissed simply by declaring "all you have here are markets at work." Market workings are themselves a form of recruitment, and markets in metropolitan areas are structured by urban political boundaries. The creation of boundaries, their fortification with land use, service delivery, and taxing powers, and the jealousy they inspire in annexation battles all testify to their importance for urban real estate markets. These factors also indicate that markets are not isolated and ineluctable in their working. Markets are integrated with social and political systems; and market outcomes are influenced not only by supply and demand, but by social forces and political volition also. Those whose intention is to dismiss information based sorting by invoking the market metaphor are actually testifying to its existence and importance.

*Market Manipulation*

Nor is it the case that by calling recruitment outcomes "market outcomes" the analysis of sorting is then deprived of its force owing to the fact that market structures are somehow immutable. It has been noted that markets themselves run on information. The actual information provided to participants in "locations" markets can be manipulated in two basic ways: (1) the manipulation of boundary lines through their creation, elimination, and alteration; and (2) the manipulation of populations within boundary lines. Manipulation of this sort alters the bases of recruitment into locations and therefore redefines the terms of association of particular settlers with populations of determinate socioeconomic characteristics.

Examples of the first kind of manipulation are not hard to imagine. For instance, when the Missouri state legislature imposed its grid system of school district definition on Missouri counties (chapter 6) it created new political boundaries and potentially altered recruitment dynamics across the state. After this action, individuals found themselves associated de facto with new populations—the populations of the newly formed school districts in which they lived. To the degree that these newly defined populations had significant socioeconomic characteristics, new information was generated and carried by political boundary systems. Confronted with this new information, settlers were presented with the necessity of deciding whether they wished to be associated with one population or another and making appropriate adjustments.

Clearly, the possibility of manipulating boundaries in this fashion presents the further potential for purposive manipulation of markets. Boundaries may be created or altered with the specific intention of including congenial groups and excluding others and thereby increasing the recruitment of favored persons and suppressing the recruitment of those who are less favored. Indeed, the City of Houston has been placed under federal court order because of its past practice of annexing areas which would maintain the white majority within the city. The inclusion of one group and the exclusion of others affects the content of messages that markets transmit.

The second type of manipulation of the information supplied by markets involves radically altering the composition of populations within political boundaries. Eliminating substantial groups within populations that bear some salient characteristic alters the overall socioeconomic identity of the jurisdiction and thus alters recruitment in ways similar to the creation, elimination, and alteration of political boundaries themselves. There have clearly been cases in which population manipulation of this type has been accomplished. Urban renewal and redevelopment programs frequently result in the elimination of neighborhoods which offer affordable housing to low income and minority residents. The elimination of the housing effectively results in the elimination of low income and minority groups as parts of jurisdictional populations in many cases. Particularly in suburban jurisdictions, the absence of housing opportunities means that low income residents must seek affordable housing in other communities. This sequence of events has been repeated often enough to produce the aphorism that equates urban renewal with negro removal. Urban renewal programs are not the only ones that work in this fashion. When new highways are routed through urban areas, right-of-ways seem to be found in low income and minority residential tracts with greater-than-random frequency.

Again, the ability to manipulate populations in this way carries the potential for the purposive manipulation of locations markets and of the information that boundaries supply to settlers. In turn, the substantive nature of the recruitment process for the relevant jurisdictions is altered. When a neighborhood housing the entire black population of a suburban municipality is razed and replaced by a shopping mall, the import of such an action cannot be entirely lost on other blacks seeking locations in the metropolitan area. The total absence of black residents in the wake of such a project may well discourage additional blacks from seeking housing in that suburb, as well as making it more attractive to whites who do not wish to have black neighbors.

Manipulations of the two general types discussed here are not endogenous to markets and therefore are not simply economic actions. They are, for the most part, political in nature. Whatever justification there may be for arguing the ethical neutrality of actions that are, considered in themselves, "simply economic", this justification surely does not extend to politics.

## The Uniquely American Politics of
## Boundary Creation

This book was begun by remarking that there are over 80,000 governments in the United States, each with its own measure of autonomy, coercive capability, and, in many cases, taxing power. Each also has its own geographic definition, and so there are over 80,000 political boundaries in the United States as well. These boundaries tend to be most profuse in metropolitan areas where population concentrations magnify problems of maintaining internal order and providing public services. This profusion of boundaries in metropolitan areas remains substantially in effect in spite of the trend toward government consolidation in recent decades. Most of the merging of governments has occurred between school districts, and more in rural and semi-rural areas than in central cities. Hence the common incidence of cities such as Houston, Kansas City, and Los Angeles which have grown past the boundaries of their original school districts and now include a good many additional districts within their city limits.

The United States is unique in many ways, but none more interesting than this peculiar governmental fertility. Unitary governmental systems obviously cannot compete against the United States in number of governments chartered, but even among the federal systems it is the clear champion. It has units of government, it would seem, for every eventuality—mosquito abatement districts, cemetary districts, street lighting districts. We not only wish to provide a unit of government for every possible function, but we are also solicitous of the interests of the smallest possible parcels. In Harris County, Texas, alone there are some 300 water districts (Perrenod 1984).

In many cases, the consequences of the existence of these separate governmental units are trivial. Tiebout to the contrary notwithstanding, it is difficult to imagine that residents of Harris County know which, specifically, of the 327 local water districts they live in or how its services or rates compare with the other 326 (Perrenod 1984; Lowery and Lyons 1989; Corzine and Stanley 1971). It is correspondingly difficult, therefore, to think that their location decisions are much influenced by the existence of units of government such as these.

Municipalities and school districts are a different matter. Citizens generally understand the importance of these governments and one can readily suppose that boundary configurations enter into their thinking when they make locational decisions. The calculus of making such decisions must be radically different for an American than it is for, say, a French citizen because the multiplicity of American political boundaries presents her with a problem of choice that the French citizen does not have. The position in this book has been that the American system of urban political boundaries conditions the decision making calculus of settlers by providing them a frame of reference, a unique system of cognitive categories which structures and carries information and, in turn, structures the locational decisions that they eventually make. This is a recruitment-based sorting process and the effectiveness of recruitment is increased because objective political boundaries stand as symbols of the political powers that can be used to maintain the community's socioeconomic composition, economic base, and life style. The outcome is what has variously been called the "mosaic culture" (Berry 1973), the "polycentric metropolis" (Ostrom et al. 1970), or the "separated metropolis" (Danielson 1976).

If it is true that the presence of such a system of cues generates a peculiar decision-making calculus, there should be differences in the settlement patterns that characterize the United States and those that are found in other countries. Specifically, there should be a higher degree of segregation by salient characteristics in the United States. No definitive work has been done on this subject, but there is anecdotal evidence to support this hypothesis. Downs, for instance, notes the differential patterns of urban settlement by poor persons in the United States and in other countries—"in many urban areas around the world where zoning and other land-use controls are not strongly enforced poor people live at all distances from the urban center, not mainly clustered near it" (1981: 41). Barry (1973: chapter 4) comments on the relative lack of segregation by race and class in Britain and Western Europe. Downs attributes this clustering of American poor to the exercise of exclusionary powers at the urban periphery, but it is clear that that exclusionary actions simultaneously transmit two messages—one to those who are excluded and a second to those who are, by implication, invited to enter.

Downs is more explicit about the impact of American governmental and boundary structure in discussing education. The nature of educational governance in the United States, he says, encourages geographic isolation by socioeconomic status.

> A second factor supporting exclusionary attitudes among high- and middle-income households is the nature of U.S. public schools. In many other nations, children from such households attend private schools, or most very poor children do not attend school at all, or *there is no strong link between where a household lives and which public school its children attend.* Therefore, households with very different income levels can live near each other without their children attending the same schools (Downs 1981: 51. Emphasis added).

The wedding of schools to circumscribed geographies, Downs argues, influences the way in which settlers think about their locations with regard to public schools.

> Until recently, except where racial segregation was legally established, nearly all U.S. children, regardless of their socioeconomic or ethnic backgrounds, attended the nearest public school. Therefore, placing neighbor-

hoods differing in average income or ethnic groups near each other at any given distance from the area's center would cause the children from all these groups to attend the same schools. Most high- and middle-income parents want their children to attend schools where other children from similar households predominate . . . Yet they also want to use public schools which are far less costly to parents. The only way they can guarantee both these conditions is to live where there are few low-income neighborhoods nearby. Thus, the nature of U.S. public schools transforms the desire of high- and middle-income households for *neighborhood* socioeconomic segregation—which is found nearly everywhere in the world—into a desire for *regional* socioeconomic segregation—which is much rarer. Recent court decisions mandating the busing of children to schools other than the ones nearest their homes reinforce this desire for regional separation by income group and race. Now the only way for a high- or middle-income household to ensure that its children will attend public schools dominated by children of similar background is to live out of practical or legal busing range of low- and moderate-income neighborhoods (Downs 1981: 51–52. Emphasis in original.)

The United States, then, is *sui generis* with regard to the sheer number of autonomous governments chartered within its borders and the boundary politics that such fragmentation engenders. This uniqueness extends to the methods by which those governments are chartered as well. I want to make the point explicitly that the proliferation of governments in the United States did not occur by divine fiat. It represents the outcomes of conscious decisions and particular circumstances. The means of chartering governments are political and, hence, the drawing and manipulation of boundaries is a political process. Urban political boundaries represent policy outcomes every bit as much as price supports or civil rights legislation. The system of urban political boundaries was created by political means, and it can, of course, be changed by political means.

What policies govern the creation of political boundaries? Teaford offers an excellent history of these policies
in the United States (Teaford 1979). He notes that the
chartering of municipalities originally required a specific
act of legislation by a state legislature. As populations
grew, however, the weight of such proposed legislation became burdensome, and state legislatures took steps to
make chartering a matter of formula. The creation of a
municipality no longer required that the legislature be directly petitioned. It was sufficient merely to meet certain
criteria—population of sufficient size and passage by
plebiscite tend to be ubiquitous.

Even these criteria, Teaford notes, tend to be more
formal than real. Legislatures rarely oppose incorporation
on the grounds of insufficient population (or even care
enough to notice such discrepancies). So it is that the metropolitan landscape is dotted with such colossi as Champ,
Missouri, population 20 (St. Louis County Department of
Planning 1982). And cases of the manipulation of incorporation referenda are well known. It is a tried-and-true
technique of American local politics to locate the required
notices of such referenda in obscure places such as the
rear of buildings along little-traveled alleys. The referen-
dum is carried by an inner-circle of apprised residents in
the midst of the majority of the population who are un-
aware of it.

Norton (1979), following Danielson (1976), also emphasizes the role of state legislatures in giving statutory
support to political fragmentation. He notes the correla-
tion between stringent state annexation laws and the
presence of "socially undesirable" groups in central cities.
The influx of Southern and Eastern Europeans to American industrial cities was met by the outmigration of the
well-to-do who were attempting to maintain status and
social distance (Norton 1979: 84). Simultaneously, legislatures in states receiving large numbers of immigrants
gave suburbs greater power to provide their own services,
made incorporation easier, and adopted double-majority
requirements for central city annexation (Norton 1979:
86). In the Northern Tier states, legislatures passed stat-

utes intended to facilitate the creation of municipal borders, and "central city borders in the industrial metropolis perform the latent function of 'containing' the urban poor" (Norton 1979: 86).

Other studies do little to refute the argument that boundary formation is pretty much a matter of citizen discretion in the United States. Miller, for instance, in his study of the politics of municipal incorporation in Los Angeles county (1981) finds that legal prohibitions did little to slow the process of incorporation. Apparatus was created to approve Lakewood-Plan incorporations consistent with the needs of the county and other communities, but it had little more than rubber-stamp status.

These circumstances prevail with regard to school districts as well as municipalities. The creation of school districts in most states does not involve the discretion of authorities. It is a matter of citizens meeting objective criteria. Stafford Independent School District in the Houston metropolitan area was created by citizens who were dissatisfied with services provided by the Fort Bend Independent School District. The Berkeley School District in St. Louis County was created by whites who wished to separate themselves from the heavily black Kinloch School District.

In effect, policies in the United States governing the creation and manipulation of political boundaries amount to a recognition of the right of any group of citizens to have their own units of government representing their peculiar interests and reflective of their socioeconomic, ethnic, and ideological character. Decisions with regard to boundaries have been left to citizens. This fact has tended to favor, to use Hirschman's terminology, exit over voice and loyalty. It encourages political fragmentation rather than community. It has given free reign to what Salisbury (1983) calls the American "hiving-off instinct."

*Anti-Government*

Indeed, it is plausible to argue that the creation of American local government is very often an act of "anti-government". The intention in creating such anti-governments is that they be used by narrowly constituted, homogeneous groups as shields against the collective political power of the remainder of American civil society, or some fraction thereof. The apparatus of suburban government—the ability to control taxation, policy, and land use locally-provides a barrier against the interests and aspirations of a more heterogeneous society. Incorporation is an act of anti-government in the sense that it permits residents to escape the collective political demands of larger, more inclusive governmental units. Government becomes, not the agency for brokering the legitimate interests of a diverse society, but an instrument for protecting parochial interests against the brokering process. It becomes a means of escaping the social contract.

There have been many perspectives on the appropriate role of government in American democracy. One sees government as a moral arena in which informed citizens seek to identify and articulate their common aspirations (Dewey, 1954). Government is the means by which civil society identifies and pursues enduring public purposes. The participation of citizens is assumed to be disinterested insofar as their votes are cast on the basis of what is best for their society rather than what will benefit them personally. In Rousseauian terms, the goal of participation is not to determine the "will of all", but the "general will", which is infallibly directed toward the common good. This view of government as an instrument of moral purpose conforms to the view that Elazar (1972) ascribes to "moralistic" political cultures.

A second view sees government as primarily an arena of power. From this perspective, government is a broker. It is the arena in which conflicting interests meet and are amalgamated. In this arena, compromises are made such that a broad diversity of interests are translated into policy, and policy is justified because it reflects the rudimentary fairness of taking many points of view into account. In this Madisonian perspective, the legitimacy of government derives from the fact that no one interest is allowed to predominate, and thus the rights of citizens are protected. This is the pluralist perspective described by Dahl (1956; Dahl and Lindblom 1953) and others; and insofar as it is predicated upon the pursuit of interest, it is compatible with what Elazar terms individualistic political culture.

A third view of the proper role of government that has been influential in the American context is the Jeffersonian view of government as the incubator of democracy. Government is the arena in which citizens learn their responsibilities, grow to understand democratic processes and institutions, and develop a patriotic devotion to them and their country. Jefferson, Mill, Dewey, and others who have taken this perspective have insisted that such government must be local—it must be immediately accessible to the citizen and be oriented toward his/her immediate concerns. The virtue of local government as an incubator of democracy is that it gives citizens autonomy over those things that impinge most frequently upon their daily lives. The incubator perspective is also predicated upon an understanding of government as a force for moral good, and is compatible with the assumptions of moralistic political culture.

One reason that local government in the United States is called anti-government is that it is deficient from all three perspectives. First, the creation of local government is more likely to be an attempt to thwart any common or collective good in favor of parochial interest. Rarely is incorporation pursued for any purpose that extends beyond corporate boundaries. Furthermore, given the common understanding in western civilization, following Kant and Rousseau, of moral behavior as *dis*interested behavior, undertaken from some motivation other than common appetite or self-interest, the creation of local government in the United States seldom qualifies as a moral act, nor is local government often mistaken for a moral arena.

Neither is local government compatible with the pluralist perspective. Incorporation is more likely to be an attempt to avoid compromise among diverse interests.

Indeed, it is usually meant to avoid diversity in order to secure or protect local advantage. In this respect, incorporation is an act of anti-politics from the point of view of pluralists such as Bernard Crick (1982), as well as being an act of antigovernment. It is an attempt to avoid dealing with competing interests by ruling competitor groups outside the realm. Incorporation is an attempt to maximize the area of political "non-decision" (Bachrach and Baratz 1962); an attempt to purify the agenda by ridding it of the problems and proposals of competitors.

Of course, any argument for the compensatory value of local government as an incubator of democrats has difficulty in overcoming one fairly devastating objection— Americans don't, by and large, participate in local government. They don't pay much attention to it, even if it embodies their most immediate political concerns, and they don't vote in local elections. They are not knowledgeable about local government. Their most frequent contact with local government is likely to be to call some local official and complain about the delivery of some service (Sharp 1984b; Verba and Nie 1972).

The creation of local government in a great many cases is not a manifestation of a desire by citizens to be closer to or more involved in the democratic life of their society, but, on the contrary, a sign that they wish to blunt, deflect, and isolate themselves from democratic processes. The creation of local government is, in fact, an act of anti-government.

Examples of incorporation in pursuit of anti-government have been widely documented. Incorporation might provide corporate interests protection against taxation and regulation (Teaford 1979; Miller 1981), or permit the upper and middle classes to escape financing public services that benefit low income citizens (Schneider 1987; Schneider and Logan 1981), or make possible the provision of public services at low tax rates, perhaps because of subsidization by residents of other cities through county taxation (Miller 1981). Miller (1981) offers the example of Industry, California. Incorporated by local businessmen, this town contains few residential areas and levies no property taxes. Industry has no official budget. Its principal reason for existing, other than protecting local corporations form annexation by larger communities in Los Angeles County, appears to be to float municipal bond issues in order to provide low-cost investment capital for local companies. Miller documents the advantages of incorporation accruing to other Lakewood Plan cities—avoidance of annexation by Los Angeles or Long Beach and the opportunity to contract for services from Los Angeles County at artificially low prices. Annexation by a heterogeneous, "full-service" central city often means that suburbanites have to pay for services that benefit principally lower income citizens (Schneider 1987).

In the 1970s, Black Jack Missouri, incorporated to gain zoning power in order to prevent the construction of low income housing (*New York Times* 1974). Residents of Black Jack feared that subsidized housing might be occupied by blacks. Miller (1981) documents the use of incorporation in Los Angeles County to protect the exclusivity of Rancho Palos Verdes, Rolling Hills, and Rolling Hills Estates (Miller 1981: 87–95).

"Skirmishes on the urban frontier" (Mowitz and Wright 1962) are typically fought over local parochial interests. They involve parties who are either seeking economic advantage or social exclusivity (Teaford 1979: 10–24). Battles over incorporation and annexation turn on considerations of tax rate, mix of services, class and race of the groups involved or affected, benefits of development and who reaps them, and implications for the character and lifestyles of communities (Mowitz and Wright 1962: 579–628). Venality is about the highest moral elevation to which such discussions rise.

The use of local government as anti-government appears to be a singularly American art, at least when the United States is compared to Western European industrial democracies (those nations to which it is most comparable). Teaford (1979) notes that local government formation in the United Kingdom is under centralized national control. Citizens are given permission to create a new unit of local government only when it has been demonstrated that overarching public purposes will be served.

Berry (1973) compares urban development in Western Europe with urban development in the United States. There are a number of important differences. Of course, Western European nations and the United Kingdom have much greater central government planning of urban development and control over developmental resources than does the United States. Urban real estate is often publicly owned, and there is no tradition of radical local autonomy over land use. In any case, national governments were forced to become involved in urban development in the wake of World War II in order to rebuild cities and replenish housing stocks. Most importantly, urban development is regarded in these countries as an integrated part of national policy. Urban planning is undertaken in the context of the pursuit of national economic and social goals. Berry notes that these goals are not entirely uniform across nations, but they typically include:

(1) *balanced welfare*—achieving a more 'balanced' distribution of income and social well-being among the various regions of the country, as well as among social classes; (2) *centralisation/decentralisation*—establishing a linked set of local and national public institutions which make it possible to develop, at the national level, overall growth strategies, integrated with regional or metropolitan planning and implementation that is partly a product of a reformed local governmental system and is directly accountable to local officials and the affected constituency; *(3) environmental protection*—channeling future growth away from areas suffering from environmental overload or which possess qualities worthy of special protection, towards areas where disruption of the environment can be minimised; (4) *metropolitan development*—promoting more satisfactory patterns of metropolitan development through new area-wide governmental bodies and the use of special land use con-

trols, new towns, housing construction, new transportation systems, and tax incentives and disincentives; (5)
*non-metropolitan development*—diverting growth into
hitherto by-passed regions by developing 'growth cen-
tres' in presently non-metropolitan regions, constructing
new transportation links between such regions and cen-
tres of economic activity, using various incentives and
disincentives to encourage or compel location of economic activity in such areas, and forcibly relocating certain government activities into them (Berry 1973: 142–
143).

In Britain and Europe, these programs have frequently increased the number of suburbs, but always in
the context of furthering national priorities. Such incorporations tend to be inclusive in spirit and execution
rather than exclusive. Private land speculation for profit
is either prohibited or closely constrained. Berry summarizes characteristics that distinguish urban development
(and local government formation) in Western Europe and
Britain from development in the United States: "public
creation of satellite communities, with consistent overall
architectural design, green belts and open space, specifi-
cation of growth directions, and clear preferences for mass
transportation, as opposed to private development of au-
tomobile oriented suburbs drifting after major style-
setting, profit seeking private initiatives" (Berry 1973:
154).

The essence of anti-government is the use of local
public power to protect parochial interests against conflicting social goals and public interests in the broader society. In other industrial democracies, parochial interests
are subordinated to broader public priorities. The United
States, however, presents a unique combination of circumstances. It is extremely heterogeneous socially, having
great diversity of social groups and interests. It has a decentralized economic system, characterized by greater inequality than other Western democracies, and predicated
upon consumer sovereignty. And it has a fragmented po-

litical system in which local government formation and policy are given over to narrow social and socioeconomic groups. The interaction of these uniquely American components produces a uniquely American outcome— anti-government is a perculiarly American practice.

*Life in the Theme Park*

The other side of the anti-government coin is the desire to live in a theme park. The theme park is, *par excellance,* a place of escape, a place where worries and cares must remain outside the gate. It is preeminently a controlled environment. Every element—the cotton candy, the landscaping, the fantastical architecture, the amusements and rides—is planned, organized to facilitate escape from the uncertainty of the real world. Danger is transformed in the theme park. The roller-coaster offers mock-danger. It presents the spectre of danger, but in a controlled situation in which one's safety is ultimately assured. The theme park caricatures life and reduces it to manageable proportions.

Many suburban municipalities approximate the theme park in offering a controlled environment. They promise pleasingly uniform architecture, coordinated, perhaps, around a central theme (Atascocita, in the Houston metropolitan area, promises the flavor of Old Spain). They promise amenities—country club membership, golf course, lakes, green space, boutiques, racket clubs, social organizations. They avoid redistributive social programs and offer services at low tax rates. They are isolated from crime, drug trafficking, and other social pathologies. The high cost of residences within the theme park and land use controls insure that exposure to undesirable socioeconomic groups will be minimized. These suburbs appeal to the preferences of middle class settlers for residential space that is secure and controlled. If one can afford the gate price, one can live in the theme park.

Essential components permitting the existence of theme park suburbs are the ability to gain planning power and land use control through incorporation, and the concomitant ability to draw a political boundary around the residential space. Power over land use assures the perpetuation of the theme park environment. The political boundary enhances place identity and stands as a bulwark against annexation. Place identity is essential for the successful recruitment of appropriate residents into the community. Political boundaries and political autonomy provide assurance to prospective settlers of continued control and isolation.

Not all suburbs, of course, are theme park suburbs. But the existence of such suburbs, even if they are in the minority, influences outcomes in other places. Sorting outcomes in places in metropolitan areas are interdependent (Downs 1981; Hirsch 1983). The disproportional recruitment of middle and upper class families into exclusive suburbs implies the simultaneous disproportional assignment of the working class and the underclass to other places. The existence of theme park suburbs, free of problems and pathologies, guarantees the existence of depressed central cities and suburbs where problems and pathologies are concentrated and predominant.

This is not to argue that sorting by race, ethnicity, and socioeconomic status would disappear in the absence of political boundaries. I agree with Lyons and Lowery (1986: 323) "that 'families with similar resources, beliefs, and habits' tend to cluster in urban space." However, when jurisdictional boundaries and the boundaries of "social worlds" correspond (Lyons and Lowery 1986), social isolation implies the compartmentalization of resources as well. Political boundaries in such situations separate resources from needs. In a more inclusive jurisdiction, resources could flow to areas beset by pathologies, deteriorating schools, and crumbling infrastructure.

Nor would sorting be likely to be as complete as it now is. At the very least, the absence of suburban anti-governments would present the middle and upper classes with a reduced incentive for exit when problems appear in neighborhoods.

## Conclusion: The Implications and Costs
## of Anti-Government

The purpose of the first six chapters of this book has been to argue that the existence of the urban political boundary system in the United States has certain implications. Its primary effect is the sorting of the population into geographically defined groups by salient characteristics such as race and socioeconomic status. The heart of this argument is the contention that urban political boundary systems have a cognitive impact. They provide cognitive categories for thinking about urban geographies. Urban political boundaries create within settlers a sense of integrated and discrete "place" where otherwise there might be none. Any sort of boundary, of course, performs this function. Political boundaries perform it particularly well for being unambiguously defined and easily accessible.

This book portrays settlers in urban areas as having preferences about locations. They wish to associate with certain types of people, to enjoy a certain lifestyle, to send their children to certain types of schools. In order to exercise these preferences, settlers must have information that can be related to urban geographies. Urban political boundaries structure information by providing cognitive categories that can be applied to geographies, and hence make it possible to identify spatial units with particular populations and the characteristics and life styles of those populations. This is the logic by which political boundaries are incorporated into sorting dynamics that result in various types of urban segregation. It has been emphasized in this chapter that the existing structure of urban boundaries is the result of policy decisions. It is easy to create governmental units in the United States and, in turn, to generate boundaries. The significance of this fact is that these boundaries then become part of the information system upon which settlers rely. Aside from the exclusionary implications of generating governments *ad infinitum,* there are implications for the recruitment dynamic that has been explored. The ability to generate additional political boundaries is also the ability to make micro-adjustments to the information system by which settlers are directed to segregated destinations.

This chapter has attempted to demonstrate that there is nothing "given" about sorting or the system of boundaries that supports it. It is not dictated by the workings of markets because markets can be readily manipulated toward certain ends. Nor can it be considered immune against human ingenuity on any other grounds because it is produced by a very human activity—politics. Settlers eventually arrive in certain locations in part because of the conscious decisions made by specific individuals within political systems.

There is a curious tendency to ignore the fact that segregative outcomes are purposive. Coleman, for instance, in his controversial study of education outcomes found that the social context of the family and the student body were more important for understanding educational achievement than were school facilities or teachers (Coleman et al. 1966). The implication is that educational opportunity is somehow a matter outside of the educational system. It is a given, something that political strategies dealing with the delivery of educational services cannot remedy.

This position ignores the fact that though these important influences on student achievement may be structured outside the schools, they are nonetheless structured within the education system. At the level of the school it appears that, in terms of the class and cultural characteristics of the students, the education system has to take what it gets. But at the level of the school district, it is apparent that decisions taken within the educational system frequently influence the class and cultural contexts within which particular students live and study. The educational system includes the boundaries of school districts. These boundaries wed a political unit to a geographic area. They are a way of "organizing political space" (Lyons and Lowery 1986). Quite frequently, they also are social boundaries, separating socioeconomic and ethnic groups from one another. This is not accidental. Research in one metropolitan area after another indicates that this congruence of political, geographic, and social boundaries is often created by decisions taken within the educational system expressly for that purpose (Orfield 1978; Dimond 1985). The cultural environment created by the association of children in schools is not a random matter, or at least not always so. It is the product of a number of social forces, one of which is discriminatory power exercised through the fragmented structure of metropolitan educational governance.

Similarly, the distribution of attitudes that children encounter in their neighborhoods are partially set by decisions made in the educational system. It would appear that the cultural context provided by the family is less amenable to direct modification by the education system. But the passivity and negativity that is generated in low status families is partly a product of the isolation of these families in depressed residential areas (Rainwater 1974; Hess 1970). To the degree that the education system contributes to this isolation, even family background is not a totally exogenous factor. The education system, then, does exert an effect on the academic achievement of children, quite possibly a more profound affect than Coleman was prepared, given the focus of his investigation, to discover.

The really pernicious aspect of sorting is this creation of varying social contexts. It is trivially true that different individuals have different experiences in, for instance, the education system. Some of these differences, however, are not random. They are structured by school district boundaries. The significance of being a black child and being surrounded in school only by other black children in a predominantly white society cannot be entirely lost on the child himself. Bowles and Gintis claim that schools "create and reinforce patterns of social class, racial, and sexual identification among students which allow them to relate 'properly' to their eventual standing in the hierarchy of authority and status in the production process"

(Bowles and Gintis 1976: 11). It has been argued here that the fragmented public education system acts in this manner by transmitting different messages to students about what is expected to them in terms of social, economic, and political participation.

Social context can have a pernicious effect in neighborhoods, obviously, as well as schools. The process of sorting in urban areas in the United States results in some neighborhoods that are bereft of resources, areas where only the most destitute live (Wilson 1987). In these areas, social pathologies are concentrated and magnified. Those who live in these areas bear the costs of these social pathologies—indeed, it can be plausibly argued that the *raison d'etre* of our politically fragmented local governmental structure is to create anti-governments, and thus to localize and impose these costs—both economic and social (Lyons and Lowery 1986; Miller 1981; Downs 1981; Sternlieb 1971; Long 1971)—on populations that have insufficient resources to transfer them back upon the white middle class. The weight of these costs is increased by the fact that persons who are socialized to the the values of low resource areas lose sight of incentives to acquire resources and escape. "Young people are discouraged from adopting attitudes toward learning and work that would enable them to escape from such conditions by developing skills marketable in the larger society" (Downs 1981: 120; see also Lemann 1986a, 1986b; Wilson 1985, 1987). Downs describes the effects of urban development in the United States in this fashion:

> But this same process is disastrous for the lowest-income households, many of whom it compels to concentrate in the oldest, most deteriorated neighborhoods. Conditions associated with poverty—unemployment, public dependency, crime, vandalism, delinquency, arson, housing abandonment, drug addiction, and broken homes—are magnified and come to dominate the entire environment. Most households with enough resources to choose other locations either refuse to move into such

neighborhoods or soon leave them. Hence these neighborhoods become occupied mainly by households who cannot move elsewhere—the least capable, least self-confident, least resourceful, least hopeful households in the entire urban area. (Downs 1981: 53)

The process of urban development in the United States is not random nor is it given. It is a process that has been structured politically. The costs of this process are imposed on that part of the population which has the fewest resources, while those that are the chief beneficiaries of the process in terms of pleasant lifestyles, good education, and quality housing bear very few costs.

This book has attempted to demonstrate that urban political boundaries are an important part of this urban development process. This argument has not been explicitly made elsewhere in the literature of urban studies. Other explanations of urban outcomes emphasize exclusionary powers that are exercised by metropolitan governments. There is no point in denying that these exclusionary powers exist and that they are responsible for a great deal of the sorting of populations that occurs in American cities. It is also clear, however, that exclusion alone cannot account for enduring segregation by race and class.

I have argued that the structure of urban political boundaries is no less important than the governments that it defines. Political boundaries support the recruitment that is the complement to exclusion in urban sorting. They are significant in themselves as a system of information, a frame of reference which provides cues to persons making locational decisions. Political boundaries are manifestations of the widespread recognition of *place*, a spatial unit with its own identity, separate and recognizeable from other spatial units. Once discrete spatial units exist they can begin to acquire attributes, and it is possible to support sorting across urban geographies. Individual preferences are matched with the attributes of place in the calculus of persons making location decisions.

Empirical evidence has been presented in Chapters Four, Five, and Six to indicate that such an information-based sorting dynamic is present in American urban centers.

In simple terms, the point of this book is that in creating numerous places numerous cells are also created within which urban populations can be segregated. This segregation, to the degree that it represents the separation of whites from blacks, lower income groups from the middle class, religious groups from one another, and so on, has been the subject of much comment. Considerable energies have been expended since World War II to create an integrated and fair society. There are a number of indications that as a people we perceive that the American model of democracy requires a citizenry in which social groups are not radically isolated from one another. I have argued that one of the instruments of group isolation has been the system of urban jurisdictional boundaries. Policy initiatives intended to produce a more integrated and tolerant society cannot be entirely successful while metropolitan areas remain spatially fractured and politically fragmented.

# References

Alcaly, Roger E., and David Mermelstein. 1976. "Preface." In *The Fiscal Crisis of American Cities,* Alcaly and Mermelstein, eds., pp. ix–xiv. New York: Vintage Books.

Anderson, Elijah. 1985. "Race and Neighborhood Transition." In *The New Urban Reality.* Paul E. Peterson, ed., pp. 92–127. Washington, D.C.: The Brookings Institution.

Anderson, Theodore R., and Janice A. Egelund. 1961. "Spatial Aspects of Social Area Analysis." *American Sociological Review* 26 (June): 392–398.

Averch, Harvey A., et. al. 1975. "How Effective is Schooling? A Critical Synthesis and Review of Research Findings." In *The Inequality Controversy: Schooling and Distributive Justice,* Donald M. Levine and Mary Jo Bane, eds., pp. 63–97. New York: Basic Books.

Babcock, Richard F. 1973. "Exclusionary Zoning: A Code Phrase for a Notable Legal Struggle." In *The Urbanization of the Suburbs,* Louis H. Masotti and Jeffery K. Hadden, eds., pp. 313–328. Beverly Hills: Sage Publications.

Bachrach, Peter. 1967. *The Theory of Democratic Elitism: A Critique.* Boston: Little, Brown, and Co.

Bachrach, Peter, and Morton Baratz. 1962. "The Two Faces of Power." *American Political Science Review,* 62 (December): 947–952.

Barker, Lucius J., and Twiley W. Barker, Jr. 1978. *Civil Liberties and the Constitution*. Englewood Cliffs, New Jersey: Prentice-Hall.

Baron, Harold M. 1969. "The Web of Urban Racism." In *Institutional Racism in America*, Louis L. Knowles and Kenneth Prewitt, eds., pp. 134–176. Englewood Cliffs, New Jersey: Prentice-Hall.

Berke, Joel S., Margaret E. Goertz, and Richard J. Coley. 1984. *Politicans, Judges, and City Schools: Reforming School Finance in New York*. New York: Russell Sage Foundation.

Berry, Brian J. L., 1973. *The Human Consequences of Urbanization*. New York: St. Martin's Press.

Berry, Brian J. L., et. al. 1976. "Attitudes toward Integration: The Role of Status in Community Response to Racial Change." In *The Changing Face of the Suburbs*, Barry Schwartz, ed., pp. 221–264. Chicago: University of Chicago Press.

Bish, Robert L. 1976. "Fiscal Equalization through Court Decisions: Policy-making without Evidence." In *The Delivery of Urban Services: Outcomes of Change*, Elinor Ostrom, ed., pp. 75–102. Beverly Hills: Sage Publications.

_____. 1971. *The Public Economy of Metropolitan Areas*. Chicago: Markham Publishing Co.

Blau, Judith R., and Peter M. Blau. 1982. "The Cost of Inequality: Metropolitan Structure and Violent Crime." *American Sociological Review* 47 (February): 114–128.

Bobo, Lawrence, Howard Schuman, and Charlotte Steeh. 1986. "Changing Racial Attitudes toward Residential Integration." In *Housing Desegregation and Federal Policy*, John M. Goering, ed., pp. 152–169. Chapel Hill, NC: University of North Carolina Press.

Boudon, Raymond. 1974. *Education, Opportunity, and Social Equality*. New York: John Wiley and Sons.

Bowles, Samuel S., and Henry M. Levin. 1968. "More on Multicollinearity and the Effectiveness of Schools." *The Journal of Human Resources* 3: (Summer): 393–400.

Bowles, Samuel S., and Herbert Gintis. 1976. *Schooling in Capitalist America: Educational Reform and the Contradictions of Economic Life.* New York: Basic Books.

Boynton, G. R. 1980. *Mathematical Thinking about Politics: An Introduction to Discrete Time Systems.* New York: Longman.

Bradbury, Katherine L., Anthony Downs, and Kenneth Small. 1982. *Urban Decline and the Future of American Cities.* Washington, D.C.: The Brookings Institution.

Burgess, Ernest W. 1967 (1925). "The Growth of the City: An Introduction to a Research Project." In *The City,* Robert E. Park, Ernest W. Burgess, and R. D. Mackenzie, eds., pp. 47–62. Chicago, University of Chicago Press.

Cain, Glen G., and Harold W. Watts. 1968. "The Controversy about the Coleman Report: Comment." *The Journal of Human Resources* 3 (Summer): 389–392.

Campbell, Alan K. (undated.) "Education in its Metropolitan Setting." In *Metropolitan School Organization, Vol I: Basic Principles and Patterns,* Troy V. McKelvey, ed., pp. 9–18. Berkeley: McCutchan.

Campbell, Alan K., and Philip Meranto. 1976 (1967). "The Metropolitan Education Dilemma: Matching Resources to Needs." In *Cities and Suburbs: Readings in Local Politics and Public Policy,* Bryan T. Downes, ed., pp. 336–351. Belmont, CA: Wadsworth Publishing Company.

Catau, John C., and J. Dennis Lord. 1981. "The School Desegregation-Resegregation Scenario: Charlotte-Mecklenburg's Experience." *Urban Affairs Quarterly* 16 (March): 369–376.

Chiang, Alpha C. 1974. *Fundamental Methods of Mathematical Economics.* New York: McGraw-Hill.

Choldin, Harvey M., and Claudine Hanson. 1982. "Status Shifts within the City." *American Sociological Review* 47 (February): 129–141.

Cion, Richard M. 1971. "Accomodation Par Excellence: The Lakewood Plan." In *Metropolitan Politics,* Michael N. Danielson, ed., pp. 272–280. Boston: Little, Brown and Co.

Cohen, Jack, Frank Falk, and Charles F. Cortese. 1976. "Reply to Taeuber and Taeuber. *American Sociological Review* 41 (August): 889–893.

Coleman, James S. 1976. "Correspondence: Response to Professors Pettigrew and Green." *Harvard Educational Review* 46 (May): 217–224.

_____. 1975. "The Concept of Equality of Educational Opportunity." In *The Inequality Controversy: Schooling and Distributive Justice,* Donald M. Levine and Mary Jo Banes, eds., pp. 199–213. New York: Basic Books.

_____. 1972. "The Evaluation of Equality of Educational Opportunity." In *On Equality of Educational Opportunity,* Frederick Mosteller and Daniel P. Moynihan, eds., pp. 146–167. New York: Vintage Books.

_____. 1968. "Equality of Educational Opportunity: Reply to Bowles and Levin." *Journal of Human Resources* 3 (Spring). 237–245.

_____. 1966. "Equal Schools or Equal Students?" *The Public Interest* 4 (Summer): 70–75.

Coleman, James S., et. al. 1966. *Equality of Educational Opportunity.* Washington, D.C.: U.S. Government Printing Office.

Coons, J. E., W. H. Clune, III, and S. D. Sugarman. 1970. *Private Wealth and Public Education.* Cambridge, MA: Belknap Press.

Cortes, Fernando, Adam Przeworski, and John Sprague. 1974. *Systems Analysis for Social Scientists.* New York: John Wiley and Sons.

Cortese, Charles F., R. Frank Falk, and Jack Cohen. 1976. "Further Considerations on the Methodological Analysis of Segregation Indices." *American Sociological Review* 41 (August): 630–637.

_____. 1978. "Understanding the Standardized Index of Dissimilarity: Reply to Massey." *American Sociological Review* 43 (August): 590–592.

Crick, Bernard. 1982. *In Defense of Politics*. New York: Penguin Books.

Dahl, Robert A. 1983. "Federalism and the Democratic Process." In *Nomos XXV: Liberal Democracy*, J. Roland Pennock and John W. Chapman, eds., pp. 95–108. New York: New York University Press.

———. 1980. "The City in the Future of Democracy." In *Urban Politics: Past, Present, and Future*, Harlan Hahn and Charles Levine, eds., pp. 339–364. New York: Longman.

———. 1956. *A Preface to Democratic Theory*. Chicago: University of Chicago Press.

Dahl, Robert A., and Edward Tufte. 1973. *Size and Democracy*. Stanford: Stanford University Press.

Dahl, Robert A., and Charles E. Lindblom. 1953. *Politics, Economics, and Welfare: Planning and Politico-economic Systems Resolved into Basic Social Processes*. New York: Harper Torchbooks.

Danielson, Michael N. 1976. *The Politics of Exclusion*. New York: Columbia University Press.

———. 1972. "Differentiation, Segregation, and Political Fragmentation in the American Metropolis." In *Governance and Population*, A. E. Keir-Nash, ed., pp. 143–176. Washington, D.C.: U.S. Government Printing Office.

Darnton, John. 1974. "The School Integration Slowdown." In *Suburbia in Transition*, Louis H. Masotti and Jeffrey K. Hadden, eds., pp. 201–207. New York: New York Times Books.

Detering, Edmund Louis. 1955. *Development of School Districts in St. Louis County with Special Emphasis on the Application of Senate Bill 307*. St. Louis: Washington University Doctoral Dissertation, Department of Education (June).

Dewey, John. 1927. *The Public and its Problems*. Chicago: The Swallow Press.

Dimond, Paul R. 1985. *Beyond Busing: Inside the Challenge to Urban Segregation*. Ann Arbor: The University of Michigan Press.

Downs, Anthony. 1985. "The Future of Industrial Cities." In *The New Urban Reality,* Paul E. Peterson, ed., pp. 281–294. Washington, D.C.: The Brookings Institution.

_____. 1981. *Neighborhoods and Urban Development.* Washington, D.C.: The Brookings Institution.

_____. 1957. *An Economic Theory of Democracy.* New York: Harper and Row Publishers.

Downes, Bryan T. 1973. "Problem Solving in Suburbia: The Basis for Political Conflict." In *The Urbanization of the Suburbs,* Louis H. Masotti and Jeffrey K. Hadden, eds., pp. 281–312. Beverly Hills: Sage Publications.

Duncan, Beverly, and Otis Dudley Duncan. 1957. *The Negro Population of Chicago: A Study of Residential Succession.* Chicago: University of Chicago Press.

Duncan, Otis Dudley, and Beverly Duncan. 1955a. "Residential Distribution and Occupational Stratification." *American Journal of Sociology* 60 (March): 493–503.

_____. 1955b. "A Methodological Analysis of Segregation Indexes." *American Sociological Review* 20 (April): 210–217.

Dye, Thomas R., et. al. 1971 (1963). "Differentiation and Cooperation in a Metropolitan Area." In *Metropolitan Politics,* Michael N. Danielson, ed., pp. 261–271. Boston: Little, Brown, and Co.

Eklund, Kent E., and Oliver P. Williams. 1978. "The Changing Spatial Distribution of Social Classes in a Metropolitan Area." *Urban Affairs Quarterly* 13 (March): 313–340.

Falk, Frank, Charles F. Cortese, and Jack Cohen. 1978. "Utilizing Standardized Indices of Residential Segregation: Comment on Winship." *Social Forces* 57 (December): 713–716.

Farley, John E. 1983. "Metropolitan Segregation in 1980: the St. Louis Case." *Urban Affairs Quarterly* 18 (March): 347–59.

Farley, Reynolds. 1977. "Residential Segregation of Urbanized Areas of the United States in 1970: An Analysis of Social Class and Racial Differences." *Demography* 14 (November): 497–518.

_____. 1976. "Componets of Suburban Population Growth." In *The Changing Face of the Suburbs,* Barry Schwartz, ed., pp. 3–38. Chicago: University of Chicago Press.

_____. 1970. "The Changing Distribuiton of Negroes within Metropolitan Areas: The Emergence of Black Suburbs." *American Journal of Sociology* 75 (January): 512–29.

Farley, Reynolds, et. al. 1978. "Chocolate City, Vanilla Suburbs: Will the Trend toward Racially Separate Communities Continue?" *Social Science Research* 7 (December): 319–44.

Feldman, Arnold S., and Charles Tilly. 1960. "The Interaction of Social and Physical Space." *American Sociological Review* 25 (December): 877–883.

Form, William H., et. al. 1954. "The Comparability of Alternative Approaches to the Delimitation of Urban Sub-areas." *American Sociological Review* 19 (August): 434–439.

Frey, Frederick W. 1971. "On Issues and Nonissues in the Study of Power." *American Political Science Review* 65 (December): 1081–1101.

Frey, William H. 1979. "Central City White Flight: Racial and Nonracial Causes." *American Sociological Review* 44 (June): 425–448.

Frieden, Bernard J. 1979. *The Environmental Protection Hustle.* Cambridge: Massachusetts Institute of Technology Press.

Friesema, H. Paul. 1973. "Cities and Suburbs and Short-lived Models of Metropolitan Politics." In *The Urbanization of the Suburbs,* Louis H. Masotti and Jeffrey K. Hadden, eds., pp. 239–252. Beverly Hills: Sage Publications.

G. and C. Merriam and Co. 1966. *Webster's Seventh New Collegiate Dictionary.* Springfield, MA: G. and C. Merriam and Co.

Goldberg, Samuel. 1957. *Introduction to Difference Equations.* New York: John Wiley and Sons.

Gordon, David. 1976. "Capitalism and the Roots of the Urban Crisis." In *The Fiscal Crisis of American Cities.* New York: Vintage Books.

Grant, Daniel R. 1971 (1964). "The Experience of Nashville's Metro." In *Metropolitan Politics,* Michael N. Danielson, ed., pp. 217–230. Boston: Little, Brown, and Co.

Greer, Scott. 1971 (1963). "The Morality Plays of Metropolitan Reform." In *Metropolitan Politics,* Michael N. Danielson, ed., pp. 160–171. Boston: Little, Brown, and Co.

Grodzins, Morton. 1957. "Metropolitan Segregation." *Scientific American* 197 (October): 33–41.

Guest, Avery M. 1971. "Retesting the Burgess Zonal Hypothesis: The Location of White Collar Workers." *American Journal of Sociology* 76 (May): 1094–1078.

Guthrie, et. al. 1971. *Schools and Inequality.* Cambridge: Massachusetts Institute of Technology Press.

Haeberle, Steven H. 1988. "Variations in Community Leaders' Subjective Definitions of Neighborhood." *Urban Affairs Quarterly* 23 (June): 616–634.

Hanushek, Eric A., and John F. Kain. 1972. "On the Value of *Equality of Educational Opportunity* as a Guide to Public Policy." In *On Equality of Educational Opportunity,* Frederick Mosteller and Daniel P. Moynihan, eds., pp. 116–145. New York: Vintage Books.

Harries, Keith D. 1974. *The Sociology of Crime and Justice.* New York: McGraw-Hill.

Harries, Keith D., and D. E. Georges-Abeyie. 1980. *Crime: A Spatial Perspective.* New York: Columbia University Press.

Hawkins, Robert B., Jr. 1976. "Special Districts and Urban Services." In *The Delivery of Urban Services: Outcomes of Change,* Elinor Ostrom, ed., pp. 171–188. Beverly Hills: Sage Publications.

Hess, Robert D. 1970. "The Transmission of Cognitive Strategies in Poor Families: The Socialization of Apathy and Underachievement." In *Psychological Factors in Poverty,* Vernon L. Allen, ed., pp. 73–92. Chicago: Markham Publishing Co.

Hill, Richard Child. 1974. "Separate and Unequal: Governmental Inequality in the Metropolis." *American Political Science Review* 19 (December): 1557–1568.

Hirsch, Arnold R. 1983. *Making the Second Ghetto: Race and Housing in Chicago, 1940–1960.* Cambridge: Cambridge University Press.

Hirschman, Albert O. 1970. *Exit, Voice, and Loyalty: Responses to Decline in Firms, Organizations, and States.* Cambridge: Harvard University Press.

Hoyt, Homer. 1939. *The Structure and Growth of Residential Neighborhoods in American Cities.* Washington, D.C.: U.S. Federal Housing Administration.

Huckfeldt, R. Robert., C. W. Kohfeld, and Thomas Likens. 1982 *Dynamic Modeling: An Introduction.* Beverly Hills: Sage Publications.

Hunt, Janet G. 1977. "Assimilation or Marginality: Some School Integration Effects Reconsidered." *Social Forces* 56 (December): 604–610.

Hunter, Albert. 1975. *Symbolic Communities: The Persistence and Change of Chicago's Local Communities.* Chicago: University of Chicago Press.

Hwang, Sean-Shong, and Steve Murdock. 1982. "Residential Segregation in Texas in 1980." *Social Science Quarterly* 63 (December): 737–748.

Jackman, Mary R. 1981. "Education and Policy Commitment to Racial Integration." *American Journal of Political Science* 25 (May): 256–269.

———. 1978. "General and Applied Tolerance: Does Education Increase Commitment to Racial Integration?" *American Journal of Political Science* 22 (May): 302–324.

Jackman, Mary, and M. J. Muha. 1984. "Education and Intergroup Attitudes: Moral Enlightenment, Superficial Democratic Commitment, or Ideological Refinement?" *American Sociological Review* 49 (December): 751–769.

Jencks, Christopher. 1973. "Inequality In Retrospect." *Harvard Educational Review* 43 (February): 138–164.

_____. 1972a. *Inequality: A Reassessment of the Effect of Family and Schooling in America.* New York: Harper Colophon Books.

_____. 1972b. "The Quality of the Data Collected by the *Equality of Educational Opportunity* Survey." In *On Equality of Educational Opportunity,* Frederick Mosteller and Daniel P. Moynihan, eds. pp. 437–512. New York: Vintage Books.

Joseph, Lawrence B. 1980. "Some Ways of Thinking about Equality of Opportunity." *Western Political Quarterly* 33 (September): 393–400.

_____. 1977. "Normative Assumptions in Educational Policy Research: The Case of Jencks' Inequality." *Annals of the American Association of Political and Social Science* 434 (November): 101–113.

Judd, Dennis R. 1979. *The Politics of American Cities: Private Power and Public Policy.* Boston: Little, Brown, and Co.

Kasarda, John D. 1985. "Urban Change and Minority Opportunities." In *The New Urban Reality,* Paul E. Peterson, ed., pp. 33–68. Washington, D.C.: The Brookings Institution.

_____. 1983. "Entry Level Jobs, Mobility, and Urban Minority Unemployment." *Urban Affairs Quarterly* 19:1 (September): 21–40.

Katznelson, Ira. 1976. *Black Men, White Cities.* Chicago: University of Chicago Press.

Kinder, Donald R. 1986. "The Continuing American Dilemma: White Resistance to Racial Change 40 Years After Myrdal." *Journal of Social Issues* 42 (2) 151–172.

Kohfeld, Carol W., and John Sprague. 1988. "Urban Unemployment Drives Urban Crime." *Urban Affairs Quarterly* 24 (December): 215–241.

Lane, Robert C. 1962. *Political Ideology: Why the American Common Man Believes What He Does.* New York: The Free Press.

Lauman, Edward O. 1966. *Prestige and Association in an Urban Community.* Indianapolis: The Bobbs-Merrill Co.

Lemann, Nicholas. 1986a. "The Origins of the Underclass, Part I." *The Atlantic* 257 (June): 31–55.

————. 1986b. "The Origins of the Underclass, Part II." *The Atlantic* 258 (July): 54–68.

Levin, Henry M. 1972. "The Case for Community Control of Schools." In *Schooling in a Corporate Society: The Political Economy of Education in America,* Martin Carnoy, ed., pp. 247–264. New York: Mckay.

————. (Undated.) "Financing Schools in a Metropolitan Context." In *Metropolitan School Organization, Volume I: Basic Problems and Patterns,* Troy V. McKelvey, ed., pp. 35–44. Berkely: McCutchan.

Lieberson, Stanley, and Donna K. Carter. 1982. "Temporal Changes and Urban Differences in Residential Segregation: A Reconsideration." *American Journal of Sociology* 88 (September): 296–310.

Lineberry, Robert L. 1980. "Mandating Urban Equality: The Distribution of Municipal Public Services." In *Urban Politics: Past, Present, and Future,* Harlan Hahn and Charles Levine, eds. pp. 173–200. New York: Longman.

Logan, John R. 1983. "The Disappearance of Communities from National Urban Policy." *Urban Affairs Quarterly* 19:1 (September): 75–90.

Logan, John R., and Linda Brewster Stearns. 1981. "Suburban Racial Segregation as a Nonecological Process." *Social Forces* 60 (September): 61–73.

Logan, John R., and Mark Schneider. 1984. "Racial Segregation and Racial Change in American Suburbs, 1970–1980." *American Journal of Sociology* 89:4 (January): 874–888.

————. 1981. "The Stratification of Metropolitan Suburbs, 1960–1970." *American Sociological Review* 46 (April): 175–186.

Long, Norton E. 1971. "The City as Reservation." *The Public Interest* 25 (Fall): 22–38.

Lowery, David, and William E. Lyons. 1989. "The Impact of Jurisdictional Boundaries: An Individual Level Test of the Tiebout Model." *Journal of Politics* 51 (February): 73–97.

Lucas, J. R. 1971. "Against Equality." In *Justice and Equality,* Hugo A. Bedau, ed., pp. 138–151. Englewood Cliffs, NJ: Prentice-Hall.

Lynch, Kevin M. 1960. *The Image of the City.* Cambridge: Massachusetts Institute of Technology Press.

Lyons, William E., and David Lowery. 1986. "The Organization of Political Space and Citizen Responses to Dissatisfaction in Urban Communities: An Integrative Model." *Journal of Politics* 48 (May): 321–346.

McClelland, D. C. 1961. *The Achieving Society.* Princeton, NJ: Van Nostrand.

Macpherson, C. B. 1977. *The Life and Times of Liberal Democracy.* Oxford: Oxford University Press.

––––––. 1962. *the Political Theory of Possessive Individualism: Hobbes to Locke.* Oxford: Oxford University Press.

Madaus, George F., et. al. 1979. "The Sensitivity of Measures of School Effectiveness." *Harvard Educational Review* 49 (May): 207–230.

Margolis, Michael, and Khondaker E. Haque. 1981. "Applied Tolerance or Fear of Government? An Alternative Interpretation of Jackman's Findings." *American Journal of Political Science* 25 (May): 241–255.

Marshall, Harvey. 1979. "White Movement to the Suburbs: A Comparison of Explanations." *American Sociological Review* 44 (December): 975–994.

Massey, Douglas S. 1978. "On the Measurement of Segregation as a Random Variable." *American Sociological Review* 43 (August): 587–589.

Massey, Douglas S., and Brendan P. Mullan. 1984. "Processes of Hispanic and Black Spatial Assimilation." *American Journal of Sociology* 89 (January): 836–873.

Massey, Douglas S., and Nancy A. Denton. 1988a. "Suburbanization and Segregation in U.S. Metropolitan Areas." *American Journal of Sociology* 94 (November): 592–626.

––––––. 1988b. "The Dimensions of Residential Segregation." *Social Forces* 67 (December): 281–315.

———. 1987. "Trends in Residential Segregation of Blacks, Hispanics, and Asians: 1970–1980." *American Sociological Review* 52 (December): 802–825.

Meade, Anthony. 1972. "The Distribution of Segregation in Atlanta." *Social Forces* 52 (December): 182–191.

Michelson, William. 1977. *Environmental Choice, Human Behavior, and Residential Satisfaction*. New York: Oxford University Press.

Mill, John Stuart. 1975. "Considerations on Representative Government." In *John Stuart Mill: Three Essays*. Oxford: Oxford University Press.

Miller, Gary J. 1981. *Cities by Contract: The Politics of Incorporation*. Cambridge: Massachusetts Institute of Technology Press.

Mogulof, Melvin B. 1971. *Governing Metropolitan Areas*. Washington, D.C.: The Urban Institute.

Molotch, Harvey Luskin. 1972. *Managed Integration: Dilemmas of Doing Good in the City*. Berkeley: University of California Press.

Morgan, Barrie S. 1982. "An Alternative Approach to the Development of a Distance Based Measure of Racial Segregation." *American Journal of Sociology* 88 (May): 1237–1249.

Mowitz, Robert J., and Deil S. Wright. 1962. *Profile of a Metropolis*. Detroit: Wayne State University Press.

Myrdal, Gunnar. 1944. *An American Dilemma: The Negro Problem and Modern Democracy*. New York: Harper and Row.

*The New York Times*. 1974 (1971). "The Justice Department v. Black Jack, Missouri." In *Suburbia in Transition*, Louis H. Masotti and Jeffrey K. Hadden, eds., pp. 158–164. New York: New York Times Books.

Norton, R. D. 1979. *City Life-Cycles and American Public Policy*. New York: Academic Press.

Okun, Arthur M. 1975. *Equality and Efficiency: The Big Trade-off*. Washington, D.C.: The Brookings Institution.

Olson, Philip. 1982. "Urban Neighborhood Research: Its Development and Current Focus." *Urban Affiars Quarterly* 17 (June): 491–518.

Orfield, Gary. 1985. "Ghettoization and its Alternatives." In *The New Urban Reality*, Paul E. Peterson, ed. pp. 161–196. Washington, D.C.: The Brookings Institution.

_____. 1978. *Must We Bus? Segregated Schools and National Policy.* Washington, D.C.: The Brookings Institution.

_____. 1976. "Federal Policy, Local Power, and Metropolitan Segregation." In *Public Power and the Urban Crisis,* Alan Shank, ed., pp.

Orlebeke, Charles. 1983. *Federal Aid to Chicago.* Washington, D.C.: The Brookings Institution.

Ostrom, Elinor. 1983. "The Social Stratification-Government Inequality Thesis Explored." *Urban Affairs Quarterly* 19:1 (September): 91–112.

_____. 1980 (1972). " Metropolitan Reform: Propositions Derived from Two Traditions." In *Urban Politics: Past, Present and Future,* Harlan Hahn and Charles Levine, eds., pp. 317–336. New York: Longman.

Ostrom, Vincent, Charles M. Tiebout, and Robert Warren. 1970 (1961). "The Organization of Government in Metropolitan Areas: A Theoretical Inquiry." *Perspectives on Urban Politics,* Jay S. Goodman, ed., pp. 98–121. Boston: Allyn and Bacon.

Palmquist, Raymond B. 1984. "Estimating the Demand for the Characteristics of Housing." *The Review of Economics and Statistics* 66 (August): 394–404.

Park, Robert E. 1952a (1936). "Succession: An Ecological Concept." In *Human Communities: The City and Human Ecology,* pp. 223–232. Glencoe, IL: The Free Press.

_____. 1952b (1929). "Sociology, Community, and Society." In *Human Communities: The City and Human Ecology,* pp. 178–209. Glencoe, IL: The Free Press.

———. 1952c (1925). "The Urban Community as a Spatial Pattern and a Moral Order." In *Human Communities: The City and Human Ecology*, pp. 165–177. Glencoe, IL: The Free Press.

Perrenod, Virginia Marion. 1984. *Special Districts, Special Purposes: Fringe Governments and Urban Problems in the Houston Area*. College Station, TX: Texas A. & M. University Press.

Peterson, Paul E. 1981. *City Limits*. Chicago: University of Chicago Press.

Pettigrew, Thomas F., and Robert L. Green. 1976a. "School Desegregation in Large Cities: A Critique of the Coleman 'White Flight' Thesis." *Harvard Educational Review* 46 (February): 1–53.

———. 1976b. "Correspondence: A Reply to Professor Coleman." *Harvard Educational Review* 46 (May): 225–233.

Prewitt, Kenneth, Sidney Verba, and Robert H. Salisbury. 1987. *An Introduction to American Government* (Fifth Edition). New York: Harper and Row.

Pryor, Frederic L. 1971. "An Empirical Note on the Tipping Point." *Land Economics* 47 (November): 413–417.

Rainwater, Lee. 1974. *What Money Buys*. New York: Basic Books.

Ross, H. Laurence. 1962. "The Local Community: A Survey Report." *American Sociological Review* 27 (February): 75–84.

Rousseau, Jean-Jacques. 1973. *The Social Contract and the Discourses*. New York: Everyman's Library.

Rubinowitz, Leonard S. 1973. "A Question of Choice: Access of the Poor and the Black to Suburban Housing." In *The Urbanization of the Suburbs*, Louis A. Masotti and Jeffrey K. Hadden, eds., pp. 329-366. Beverly Hills: Sage Publications.

Salisbury, Robert H. 1983. "The Local Community in the Federal System" (Department of Political Science Working Paper). St. Louis: Washington University.

_____. 1971. "Interests, Parties, and Government Structures in St. Louis." In *Cities and Suburbs: Selected Readings in Local Politics and Public Policy,* Bryan T. Downes, ed., pp. 201–210. Belmont, CA: Wadsworth Publishing Co.

_____. 1970. "Urban Politics: The New Convergence of Power." In *Perspectives on Urban Politics,* Jay S. Goodman, ed., pp. 38–60. Boston: Allyn and Bacon.

Schaar, John H. 1967. "Equality of Opportunity and Beyond." *Nomos IX: Equality,* J. Roland Pennock and John W. Chapman, eds., pp. 228–249. New York: Atherton Press.

Schattschneider, E. E. 1975. *The Semisovereign People: A Realist's View of Democracy in America.* Hinsdale, IL: The Dryden Press.

Schelling, Thomas C. 1978. *Micromotives and Macrobehavior.* New York: W. W. Norton and Co.

Schmandt, Henry J., George D. Wendel, and E. Allan Tomey. 1983. *Federal Aid to St. Louis.* Washington, D.C.: The Brookings Institution.

Schmid, Calvin F. 1960a. "Urban Crime Areas: Pt. I." *American Sociological Review* 25 (August): 527–541.

_____. 1960b. "Urban Crime Areas: Pt. II." *American Sociological Review* 25 (October): 655–678.

Schnare, Ann B. 1980. "Trends in Residential Segregation by Race: 1960–1970." *Journal of Urban Economics* 7 (May): 293–301.

Schneider, Mark. 1985. "Suburban Fiscal Disparities and the Location Decisions of Firms." *American Journal of Political Science* 29 (August): 587–605.

_____. 1987. "Income Homogeneity and the Size of Suburban Government." *Journal of Politics* 49 (February): 36–53.

Schneider, Mark, and John R. Logan. 1982. "Suburban Racial Segregation and Black Access to Local Public Resources." *Social Science Qyarterly* 63 (December): 762–770.

_____. 1981. "Fiscal Implications of Class Segregation: Inequalities in the Distribution of Public Goods and Services in

Suburban Municipalities." *Urban Affairs Quarterly* 17 (September): 23–36.

Schnore, Leo F. 1972. *Class and Race in Cities and Suburbs.* Chicago: Markham Publishing Co.

———. 1971 (1963). "The Social and Economic Characteristics of American Suburbs." In *Cities and Suburbs: Selected Readings in Local Politics and Public Policy,* Bryan T. Downes, ed., pp. 49–57. Belmont, CA: Wadsworth Publishing Co.

Schnore, Leo F., Carolyn D. Andre, and Harry Sharp. 1976. "Black Suburbanization 1930–1970." In *The Changing Face of the Suburbs,* Barry Schwartz, ed., pp. 69–94. Chicago: University of Chicago Press.

Schultze, Charles L., et. al. 1976. "Fiscal Problems of Cities." In *The Fiscal Crisis of American Cities,* Roger E. Alcaly and David Mermelstein, eds., pp. 189–122. New York: Vintage Books.

Schuman, Howard, Charlotte Steeh, and Lawrence Bobo. 1985. *Racial Attitudes in America: Trends and Interpretations.* Cambridge: Harvard University Press.

Schuman, Howard, and Lawrence Bobo. 1988. "Survey Based Experiments on White Racial Attitudes toward Residential Integration." *American Journal of Sociology* 94 (September): 273–299.

Scott, Stanley, and John Corzine. 1971. "Special Districts in the San Francisco Bay Area." In *Metropolitan Politics,* Michael N. Danielson, ed., pp. 246–271. Boston: Little, Brown and Co.

Scott, Thomas M. 1973. "Suburban Governmental Structures." In *Urbanization of the Suburbs,* Louis H. Masotti and Jeffrey K. Hadden, eds., pp. 213–238. Sage Publications.

———. 1971. "Metropolitan Governmental Reorganization Proposals." In *Cities and Suburbs: Selected Readings in Local Politics and Public Policy,* Bryan T. Downes, ed. pp. 441–452. Belmont, CA: Wadsworth Publishing Co.

Semyonov, Moshe, and Richard Ira Scott. 1983. "Industial Shifts, Female Employment, and Occupational Differentiation: A Dynamic Model for American Cities." *Demography* 20 (May): 136–176.

Sharp, Elaine B. 1984a. "'Exit, Voice, and Loyalty' in the Context of Local Government Problems." *Western Political Quarterly* 37 (March): 67–83.

———. 1984b. "Citizen Demand Making in the Urban Context." *American Journal of Political Science* 28 (November): 655–670.

Shaw, C. R., and H. D. McKay. 1969. *Juvenile Delinquency and Urban Areas.* Chicago: University of Chicago Press.

Shevky, Eshref, and Marilin Williams. 1949. *The Social Areas of Los Angeles.* Berkeley: University of California Press.

Shevky, Eshref, and Wendell D. Bell. 1955. *Social Area Analysis.* Stanford: Stanford University Press.

Skogan, Wesley. 1977. "The Changing Distribution of Big City Crime." *Urban Affiars Quarterly* 13 (September): 33–48.

Smith, Marshal S. 1972. "Equality of Educational Opportunity: The Basic Findings Reconsidered." In *On Equality of Educational Opportunity,* Frederick S. Mosteller and Daniel P. Moynihan, eds., pp. 230–342. New York: Basic Books.

Smith Terence, and W. A. V. Clark. 1980. "Housing Market Search: Information Constraints and Efficiency." In *Residential Mobility and Public Policy,* W. A. V. Clark and Eric G. Moore, eds., pp. 100–125. Beverly Hills: Sage Publications.

Sniderman, Paul M., and Philip E. Tetlock. 1986a. "Symbolic Racism: Problems of Motive Attribution in Political Analysis." *Journal of Social Issues* 42 (2): 173–187.

Sofen, Edward. 1971 (1963). "Reflections on the Creation of Miami's Metro." In *Metropolitan Politics,* Michael N. Danielson, ed., pp. 205–216. Boston: Little, Brown, and Co.

Sorenson, T., K. E. Taeuber, and L. J. Hollingsworth. 1974. "Indexes of Racial Residental Segregation for 109 Cities in the United States, 1940 to 1970." Institute for Research on Poverty Discussion Paper, University of Wisconsin.

Spitz, David. 1977. "A Grammar of Equality." In *The New Conservatives: A Critique from the Left,* Lewis A. Coser and Irving Howe, eds., pp. 124–150. New York: New American Library.

Sprague, John. 1981. "One Party Dominance in Legislatures." *Legislative Studies Quarterly* 6 (May): 259–286.

———. 1976. "Comments on Mobilization Processes Represented as Difference Equations or Difference Equation Systems." St. Louis: Department of Political Science Working Paper, Washington University.

———. 1969. "A Nonlinear Difference Equation." St. Louis: Department of Political Science Working Paper, Washington University.

Stahura, John M. 1988. "Changing Patterns of Suburban Racial Composition, 1970–1980." *Urban Affairs Quarterly* 23 (March): 448–460.

Stearns, Linda Brewster, and John R. Logan. 1986. "Measuring Trends in Segregation: Three Dimensions, Three Measures." *Urban Affairs Quarterly* 22 (September): 125–150

Stein, Robert M. 1987. "Tiebout's Sorting Hypothesis." *Urban Affairs Quarterly* 23 (September): 140–160.

Steinnes, Donald M. 1977. "Alternative Models of Neighborhood Change." *Social Forces* 55 (June): 1043–1057.

Sternlieb, George. 1971. "The City as Sandbox." *The Public Interest* 25 (Fall): 14–21.

Sternlieb, George, and James W. Hughes. 1976. "Metropolitan Decline and Interregional Job Shifts." In *The Fiscal Crisis of American Cities,* Roger E. Alcaly and David Mermelstein, eds., pp. 145–164. New York: Vintage Books.

Stinchcombe, Arthur L., Mary Sexton Mcdill, and Dollie R. Walker. 1969. "Is There a Racial Tipping Point in Changing Schools?" *Journal of Social Issues* 25 (January): 127–136.

———. 1968. "Demography of Organizations." *American Journal of Sociology* 74 (November): 221–229.

Suttles, Gerald D. 1972. *The Social Construction of Communities*. Chicago: University of Chicago Press.

Taeuber, Karl E. 1968. "The Effect of Income Redistribution on Racial Residential Segregation." *Urban Affairs Quarterly* 4 (September): 5–14.

Taeuber, Karl E., and Alma F. Taeuber. 1976. "A Practitioner's Perspective on the Index of Dissimilarity." *American Sociological Review* 41 (October): 884–888.

_____. 1965. *Negroes in Cities*. Chicago: Aldine.

Taub, Richard P., D. Garth Taylor, and Jan D. Dunham. 1984. *Paths of Neighborhood Change*. Chicago: University of Chicago Press.

Teaford, John C. 1979. *City and Suburb: The Political Fragmentation of Metropolitan America, 1850–1970*. Baltimore: John Hopkins University Press.

Thurow, Lester C. 1973. "Proving the Absence of Positive Associations." *Harvard Educational Review* 43 (February): 106–112.

_____. 1972. "Education and Economic Equality." *The Public Interest* 28 (Summer): 66–81.

Tiebout, Charles M. 1956. "A Pure Theory of Local Expenditures." *Journal of Political Economy* 64 (October): 416–424.

Van Valey, Thomas L., Wade Clark Roof, and Jerome E. Wilcox. 1977. "Trends in Residential Segregation: 1960–1970." *American Journal of Sociology* 82 (January): 826–844.

Verba, Sidney, and Norman Nie. 1972. *Participation in America: Political Democracy and Social Equality*. New York: Harper and Row.

Voss, H. L., and D. M. Peterson, eds. 1971. *Ecology, Crime and Delinquency*. New York: Meredith Corporation.

Walzer, Michael, 1980. "Democratic Schools." In *Radical Principals: Reflections of an Unreconstructed Democrat*, pp. 257–272. New York: Basic Books.

White, Michael J. 1983. "The Measurement of Spatial Segregation." *American Journal of Sociology* 88 (March): 1008–1018.

Wikstrom, Nelson. 1977. *Councils of Governments: A Study in Political Incrementalism.* Chicago: Nelson Hall.

Williams, Barbara R. 1973. *St. Louis: A City and its Suburbs.* Santa Monica, Ca: The Rand Corporation.

Williams, Oliver P. 1980 (1967). "Life-style Values and Political Decentralization in Metropolitan Areas." In *Urban Politics: Past, Present, and Future,* Harlan Hahn and Charles Levine, eds., pp. 201–212. New York: Longman.

Williams, Oliver P., et. al. 1971 (1965). "Suburban Attitudes, Opinions, and Local Policies." *Cities and Suburbs: Selected Readings in Local Politics and Public Policy,* Bryan T. Downes, ed., pp. 147–160. Belmont, CA: Wadsworth Publishing Co.

Wilson, William Julius. 1987. *The Truly Disadvantaged: The Inner City, the Underclass, and Public Policy.* Chicago: University of Chicago Press.

———. 1985. "The Urban Underclass in Advanded Industrial Society." In *The New Urban Reality,* Paul E. Peterson, ed., pp. 129–160. Washington, D.C.: The Brookings Institution.

Winsberg, Morton D. 1983. "Changing Distribution of the Black Population, Florida Cities, 1970–1980." *Urban Affairs Quarterly* 18 (March): 361–370.

Winship, Christopher. 1977. "A Reevaluation of Indices of Segregation." *Social Forces* 55 (June): 1058–1066.

Wise, Arthur E. 1967. *Rich Schools, Poor Schools: The Promise of Equal Educational Opportunity.* Chicago: University of Chicago Press.

Wolfinger, Raymond E., and Stephen Rosenstone. 1980. *Who Votes.* New Haven: Yale University Press.

Wood, Robert C. 1970 (1961). "The Political Economy of a Metropolitan Area." In *Perspective on Urban Politics,* Jay S. Goodman, ed., pp. 27–37. Boston: Allyn and Bacon.

Ying Cheng Kiang. 1968. "The Distribution of Ethnic Groups in Chicago." *American Journal of Sociology* 74 (November): 292–295.

## Government Publications

U.S. Bureau of the Census. 1983a. *Census of Governments: Vol. 1, Governmental Organization.* Washington D.C.: U.S. Government Printing Office.

————. 1983b. *1980 Census of Population and Housing: Chicago, Ill.,* Standard Metropolitan Statistical Area, Section I. Washington, D.C.: U.S. Government Printing Office.

————. 1983c. *1980 Census of Population and Housing: St. Louis, Mo.-Ill.* Standard Metropolitan Statistical Area, Section I. Washington, D.C.: U.S. Government Printing Office.

————. 1972. *1970 Census of Population and Housing: Chicago, Ill.,* Standard Metropolitan Statistical Area. Washington, D.C.: U.S. Government Printing Office.

————. 1962. *U.S. Censuses of Population and Housing: 1960, Chicago, Ill.,* Standard Metropolitan Statistical Area. Washington, D.C.: U.S. Government Printing Office.

Saint Louis County Council. 1952. *Order of the St. Louis County Council.* Clayton, Missouri: County Government Center (April 16).

————. 1951. *Order of the St. Louis County Council.* Clayton, Missouri: County Government Center (May 1).

Saint Louis County Department of Education. 1955. *Fourth Annual Report of the St. Louis County, Missouri Public Schools to the County Board of Education for the School Year 1954–55.* Clayton, Missouri: County Government Center (November 1).

————. 1951. Minutes of Meeting no. 44. Clayton, Missouri: County Government Center (April 12).

Saint Louis County Department of Planning. 1982. *Fact Book/ 1982: St. Louis County.* Clayton, Missouri: County Government Center.

U.S. Commission on Civil Rights. 1977. *School Desegregation in Kirkwood Missouri: A Staff Report of the U.S. Commission on Civil Rights.* Washington, D.C.: U.S. Government Printing Office.

## Planning Documents

Daly, Leo A., Company. 1969. *Comprehensive Plan: Wellston, Missouri.* City Clerk, Wellston, Missouri (December).

General Planning and Resource Consultants. 1969. *A Comprehensive Community Plan: Creve Ceour, Missouri.* Creve Coeur, MO: Creve Coeur Planning and Zoning Commission (March).

Harland Bartholomew and Associates. 1969a. *The Comprehensive Plan: Frontenac, Missouri.* Frontenac, MO: City Planning Commission (March).

_____. 1969b. *Final Report upon Comprehensive Plan, Bridgeton, Missouri.* Bridgeton, MO: City Clerk (June).

Layton, Layton, and Associates. 1970. *Shrewsbury, Missouri: Comprehensive Community Plan.* Shrewsbury, MO: City Hall (March).

Office of Planning, Missouri Department of Community Affairs. 1971. *Comprehensive Plan for Hazelwood, Missouri.* Hazelwood, MO: City Planning Commission (June).

St. Louis County Department of Planning. 1974. *Comprehensive Plan: City of St. John.* Clayton, MO: County Government Center (June).

_____. 1971. *Hazelwood School District: Requirements for the Seventies.* Clayton, MO: County Government Center (December).

_____. 1970. *Rockwood R–6: A Report to the Rockwood R–6 School District.* Clayton, MO: County Government Center (May).

Saint Louis County Planning Commission. 1968. *The Parkway Planning Area: An Analysis.* Clayton, MO: County Government Center (February).

## Cases

*Acevedo v. Nassau County, New York,* 369 F. Supp. 1384 (1974).

*Alexander v. Holmes County Board of Education,* 396 U.S. 19 (1969).

*Arlington Heights v. Metropolitan Housing Development Corporation,* 429 U.S. 252 (1977).

*Bolling v. Sharpe,* 347 U.S. 497 (1954).

*Brown, et al., v. Board of Education,* 347 U.S. 483 (1954).

*Brown v. Board of Education II,* 349 U.S. 294 (1955).

*Cooper v. Aaron,* 358 U.S. 1, (1958).

*Dayton Board of Education v. Brinkman,* 97 S. Ct. 2766 (1977).

*Gilmore v. City of Montgomery, Alabama,* 417 U.S. 356 (1974).

*Griffin v. Prince Edward County School Board,* 377 U.S. 241 (1964).

*Heart of Atlanta Motel v. United States,* 379 U.S. 241 (1964).

*Hills v. Gautreaux,* 425 U.S. 284 (1975).

*Hobson v. Hansen,* 269 F. Supp. 407 (1967).

*Hurd v. Hodge,* 334 U.S. 24 (1948).

*James v. Valtierra,* 402 U.S. 137 (1971).

*Jones V. Mayer,* 392 U.S. 294 (1964).

*Katzenbach v. McClung,* 379 U.S. 294 (1964).

*Keyes v. School District No. 1, Denver, Colorado,* 413 U.S. 189 (1973).

*Liddell, et al. v. Board of Education of St. Louis,* Federal District Court, Eastern District of Missouri, cause no. 72–100c (c) (1972).

*Mahaley v. Cuyahoga Metropolitan Housing Authority,* 355 F. Supp. 1257 (1973).

*Milliken v. Bradley,* 94 Sup. Ct. 3112 (1974).

*Muir v. Louisville Park Theatrical Association,* 347 U.S. 397 (1954).

*North Carolina State Board of Education v. Swann,* 402 U.S. 43, (1971).

*Rogers v. Paul,* 382 U.S. 198 (1965).

*San Antonio Independent School District v. Rodriguez,* 411 U.S. 1 (1973).

*Shelley v. Kraemer,* 334 U.S. 1 (1948).

*Simkins v. City of Greensboro,* 149 F. Supp. 562, M.D., N.C. (1957).

*Swann v. Charlotte–Mecklenburg Board of Education,* 402 U.S. 1 (1971).

*United States v. Northwest Louisiana Restaurant Club,* 256 F. Supp. 151, W.D. La. (1966).

*United States v. Jefferson County Board of Education,* 372 F. 2d 836 (1966).

*Village of Belle Terre v. Borass,* 416 U.S. 1 (1974).

*Ybarra v. Town of Los Altos Hills,* 370 F. Supp. 742 (1973).

# Index